The Rosary in
Space and Time

The Rosary in Space and Time

Ruth Rees

GRACEWING

LITURGY
TRAINING
PUBLICATIONS

First published in 2004
jointly by

Gracewing
2 Southern Avenue,
Leominster
Herefordshire HR6 0QF

Liturgy Training Publications
Archdiocese of Chicago
1800 North Hermitage Avenue
Chicago IL 60622-1101

NIHIL OBSTAT   Monsignor G. Chidgey, Prot. Ap., J. C. D.
                Censor
IMPRIMATUR   Most Revd. Peter Smith, LL.B., J. C. D.

Date   7 June 2004

The *Nihil Obstat* and *Imprimatur* are official declarations that
a book or pamphlet is free of doctrinal error. No implication
is contained therein that those who have granted the *Nihil
Obstat* and *Imprimatur* necessarily recommend or endorse the
book or pamphlet.

UK ISBN 0 85244 610 1
USA ISBN 1-56854-564-9

Typeset by Action Publishing Technology Ltd,
Gloucester GL1 5SR

Printed in England by Antony Rowe Ltd,
Chippenham, Wiltshire SN14 6LH

Dedicated with love to the Holy Family

Contents

Foreword

The rector of the novitiate where I studied to become a Jesuit brother was a rough, gruff old priest who'd travelled around the world, facing down challenges spiritual and temporal, with a no-nonsense practicality. One day he described to us his first mission overseas, an assignment to build a high school in rural Chile. He'd arrived as a young priest with only a rudimentary knowledge of the language and local culture, and he had no experience of putting a school together.

He told us he was terrified. 'I was at such a loss of what to do, that I actually got down on my knees and prayed the Rosary.' We laughed, because we knew exactly what he meant. For all our developing talents in meditation and the Spiritual Exercises, it was reassuring for us novices to remember that the tried and trusted prayers of our childhood still worked.

Alas, too few youngsters today are taught how to pray the Rosary. They dismiss it as just a mechanical repetition of prayers, suited only for the unimaginative. But in fact it is just the opposite. It is the foundation and launch pad for the deepest kind of meditation.

Yes, the Rosary is mechanical. You could write it as a computer programme. They are prayers many have known since childhood, repeated over and over, the beads and the chain they're strung on making a firm impression as they pass through our fingers. It is a rote, it is mechanical, it is physical. That is the whole idea. We are material people, living in a material world. We must start with the physical; we must start with our senses. The recitation of the rosary for that very reason grabs our ears and tongue and fingers and sets them busy with the physical task of praying, in order to focus our imaginations and spirits on the mysteries attached to those prayers.

This mixture of the physical and the spiritual is a constant theme in my own life as a Jesuit brother and astronomer. I study the physical universe as a way of getting closer to the One who created it. I live a life where spirituality is both real and practical. I know that the physical universe, with its black holes and dark matter, is far stranger than the mundane worries of running errands and finding supper; yet without supper, the life of the mind would be cut short quickly.

Why do I pray the Rosary? Because it works. It has never failed to calm and center me; yes it was there when I needed it, when shocks shook my world – from losing a close friend, to losing the World Trade Center – and other kinds of prayer seemed impossible. But it has also given me moments when God was tangibly present in a way both good and terrifying. ('Fear of the Lord' is no idle threat!)

My friend Ruth is calling this book *The Rosary in Space and Time*, and she's exactly right. It is this fixation in space and time – not only the physical space and time where we pass the beads through our hands, but more importantly the specific space and time where occurred the mysteries that we contemplate – that is the genius and glory of Christianity.

Every religion wants to worship God 'out there' or God 'right here', God Transcendent or God Immanent. But only Christianity has what the theologians call 'the scandal of the particular': that along with 'out there' and the 'right here', we also have God Incarnate in a particular place and a particular time, doing particular things with particular people. Christ did not come to save 'humanity'; he came specifically to save me; and you, and that guy on the train this morning, chewing gum, who took the seat I had my eye on.

The four sets of mysteries are each specific incidents as historically real as our birthdays or our favourite team's last championship. It is part of the human experience to relive the high points in our histories, national or personal, until the reliving becomes itself part of who we are. And in just such a way, in meditating the mysteries of the Rosary, the acts of Mary, of the Magi, of Pilate and Peter and of the disciples who witnessed the Transfiguration, and the triumph of the cross, become a part of our experience as well.

There is one other meaning the Rosary has for me, however. It is a universal prayer uniting Catholics, liberal and conservative, simple and sophisticated, with the power to break down fears and prejudices across lines of culture or nationality.

As a member of the Vatican Observatory, working in the Pope's summer home in Castel Gandolfo, it has been my privilege to meet His Holiness on a number of occasions. The general pattern of such audiences is that, at the end, everyone present is greeted by the Pope, who hands a Rosary to that person as a memento of the visit.

One summer, soon after one of these audiences, I was visiting the Jesuit parish in Johannesburg, South Africa. While I was there, I asked the priest if it would be possible to get outside the city at night so I could get a look at the southern skies with the little telescope I'd brought along. He knew a parishioner who worked in town during the week but drove back to his farm in the countryside over the weekend, and arranged for me to ride out with him overnight.

The elderly farmer was clearly suspicious of me. To him I looked like a young bearded Jesuit scientist more interested (he suspected) in the Southern Cross than in the crucifix. As we drove on the highway out of town, he said, 'Every Friday as I drive home, I like to pray the Rosary. Would you care to join me?' He said it like a challenge. This was clearly a test. 'I would be very happy to,' I replied, and reached into my jacket pocket. 'The Pope gave me this Rosary just last week.' He smiled. We prayed together. The Rosary passed the test.

Brother Guy Consolmagno SJ, Specola Vaticana, and Vatican Observatory Research Group, Steward Observatory, University of Arizona.

Acknowledgements

Among the many people who over the years have given me so much support, advice and friendship during this labour of love, I am especially indebted to Anna Haycraft whose brilliance as my book's original editor almost matches that of her alter ego's novels; Father Andrew Wadsworth, who managed to find time in his busy life as Catholic Chaplain at Harrow School, and the demands of his own theological writings, cheerfully found time to vet every line of my MS to ensure I hadn't created any new heresies; Brother Guy Consolmagno SJ, my favourite astronomer, who with enormous good humour kept a beady and expert eye on my incursions into Space and Quantum Physics; Dom Bernard Orchard OSB, of Ealing Abbey, whose biblical expertise never fails to awe me and who had always been there when I had any Old or New Testament queries; Victoria Holdsworth of the Foreign Press Association; Jim Elliott; Stuart Mason for his splendid photograph of my rosary, and to the editors at Gracewing for their invaluable professionalism.

I am also deeply grateful to the following eminent scientists for their permission to use extracts from their inspirational comments (detailed in Part 1, Chapter 1) on television, radio and in lectures respectively: Dr Monica Grady, Curator, Meteorite Collection and Head of Petrology Meteoritics at the Natural History Museum; Russell Stannard, Professor Emeritus of Physics at the Open University, and Reader in the Church of England; and

Professor John Polkinghorne, Fellow of Queen's College, Cambridge, Anglican priest and Canon Theologian of Liverpool Cathedral. My gratitude too to Fr Colomba Ryan OP and Fr John Farrell OP of St Dominic's Priory in London, for finding time to broaden my knowledge of the Dominican Order generally and St Dominic specifically, which reinforced my delight at having been instructed in the Faith by the Dominicans in England and South Africa, so many years ago; and to the Coptic Orthodox Church Centre for their co-operation in adding to my information about the probable route taken by the Holy Family in Egypt. Dr Dan Levene, Lecturer in Jewish History and Culture at the University of Southampton, and Dr Carol Downer, both of whom shed light on the relationship between Aramaic and Hebrew; and to Professor Stephen Hawking for his courteous response to my loaded question.

Thank you all.

Introduction

The idea for this book came to me in one of the loveliest spots on earth – Agua Blava, a quiet little Mediterranean bay on the remoter, northern side of Spain's Costa Brava.

After a day relaxing in the sun, walking through pine trees, wild flowers and sweet-smelling herbs or climbing up narrow steps carved into the series of rugged promontories that jut out into the silky blue sea, I would return to the family hotel where I was staying and, overwhelmed by the beauty of God's creation, I thought that a suitable way to express my gratitude would be to pray the Rosary in thanksgiving.

Prayer has always been an important part of my life even as a child, yet after becoming a Catholic in my late 20s, I struggled with the Rosary. Over the past seven hundred years, thousands of books have been written about it; some by lay people, some by priests and members of religious Orders, and some by saints (I will touch upon that latter point later), and while some have been modest little publications, others have been expensively-produced works containing beautiful colour plates and illustrations. But nowhere did I find answers to the numerous questions that arose in my mind as I tried to meditate on each Mystery.

A few examples: what would it have been like for a Jewish family – the Holy Family – living in Roman-occupied Judea in the first century AD? Their food, homes, travels (remember that Mary was three months pregnant when she made the long journey home from her visit to Elizabeth; what form of transport would she have used?). What happened to the apostles after the resurrection? And following the death of Jesus, would traditional Jewish mourning customs have been observed? Lack of information that covered every Mystery soon became a major obstacle in my attempts at meditation, and I subsequently discovered that many people praying the Rosary experience the same difficulty.

The crisis point came following an incident which involved life and death (not my own, as I shall explain in Chapter 3) after which I made a vow to pray the Rosary every day rather than just when the mood took me, but as I tried to concentrate on the various Mysteries, I realized that for me to pray the Rosary with understanding, some sort of total immersion into a learning process was needed; but the solution only hit me during my stay in Agua Blava – I would have to use the methods of my own working background and go into investigative-journalist mode. So for the rest of my time there I wrote the first draft of this book, including a preliminary though seemingly endless list of queries that had arisen (and continued to arise) in my mind.

That was many years ago, and because of my pressurized working life, which involved a great deal of travel abroad, it was impossible until much later to embark on the sustained and lengthy research required. Fortunately, the implications of what I was undertaking did not sink in on that Spanish afternoon, or I might have been too intimidated to begin. But it has been an exciting adventure, following up the merest threads of clues which sometimes yielded just a tiny but vital part of the larger pattern, which more often than not would throw up a new set of questions that demanded further research into sources both ancient and modern. Above all, it has made me realize that it is impossible to experience the profundity of the Rosary – and pray it well and lovingly – without a close attachment to its original source: the New Testament.

A great personal joy to me in writing this book is that as a Jewish convert to the Faith, it has been thrilling to encounter familiar Jewish customs that would have been a normal part of the Holy Family's day-to-day existence as well as that of Christ's Jewish disciples as they preached the Kingdom of God.

What, the reader may ask, does the title mean: *The Rosary In Space and Time*? Well, running parallel with the above aspects of my book is my conviction that the unimaginable power of prayer generally needs to be restated, to include certain aspects of modern physics which seem to have parallels with aspects of prayer, so it has been a source of delight to learn that so many brilliant scientists in the past were, and present scientists also are, devout Christians.

Also heartening has been the increasing worldwide interest about prayer generally and the Rosary specifically, and not just among Catholics but among many Christian denominations too, for there appears to be a long-delayed recognition that the main purpose of this method of prayer to Mary is to focus our attention on Christ. As she put it so precisely herself in the Magnificat: 'My soul doth magnify the Lord ...'

Finally, referring to my earlier comment: many books have been written by saints apparently for saints. Mine has been written by a sinner for sinners. This is not a pseudo-modest attempt to be user-friendly; it is a fact.

PART I

PRAYER GENERALLY

1

Outer Space

An American friend of mine, a Jesuit astronomer and author – who spends part of the year studying meteorites at the Vatican Observatory, and the rest with its Research Group at the University of Arizona – once remarked how significant it is that the great flowering of Christian mysticism in the mediaeval era coincided with the time when astronomy was part of the educational system. Significant, yes; surprising, no; because there is a powerful link between the enigma of the visible universe and the response it evokes in the invisible depths of the human spirit. It is therefore both timely and imaginative of the decision-makers that in 1990, for the first time in British schools, astronomy became part of the core science curriculum. All we have to do now is wait for a second flowering of Christian mysticism. But that may take longer.

Of course, our mediaeval forebears had one great advantage over us – they had no effective street lighting. But even as recently as the mid-twentieth century our road lighting was much dimmer than it is now, and I doubt that I am the only Londoner who remembers the wonder felt as a tiny child looking up at starry skies. Later, as a teenager living in the beautiful Oxfordshire countryside, I used to go stargazing on my local Chiltern Hill, thinking about what I had recently learnt: that we live on a planet on the far outer rim of the Milky Way, a spiral galaxy containing some 100 billion stars and which takes 200 million years to complete a single revolution around its own centre. (At the last count, there were some 150 million other galaxies with an unimaginable number of their own stars, as well as numerous bits and pieces of cosmic matter, floating, exploding and whirling around our expanding universe.) It astonished me then, and it still astonishes me. Generally, though, it's only too easy to be lulled into a false sense of security by the cosiness of our protective blue sky, or low grey cloud, as the case and place may be, and to ignore what is happening out there in the black vacuum of outer space.

Looking at a clear night sky, we catch a glimpse of the wonders beyond daylight, yet as we race around worrying about our personal problems and trying to cope with the increasing strains of daily life in a frenetic world, how much thought do we give to the alarming, beautiful immensity of the universe? The irritated response to such a question may well be, 'Thanks, but I've got more important things to worry about'. Though to anyone under stress, I can recommend an instant antidote: find someone with a telescope and look at Saturn with its shimmering rings; it helps to put things into perspective.

For years, some scientists have arrogantly claimed it was ludicrous to suppose there could be other planetary systems apart from our own, yet at the time of going to print, a hundred planets have been discovered in orbits around dwarf stars, and by the time you read this book it is highly likely that figure will have increased. They spoke scathingly too about 'fantasies' of space travel: one, a well-known science journalist wrote in his weekly column that it was 'impossible' to put a man on the moon. Around the same time, the then Astronomer Royal, Professor Richard van der Riet Woolley, said that talk about the future of interplanetary travel was 'utter bilge ... it is all rather rot'.

Closed minds were jolted open in 1969 when men first stepped on the Moon; but not only ongoing discoveries in astronomy, but also discoveries in quantum physics, indicate that the third millennium is going to be an era that will overturn a number of hitherto scientific 'certainties'.

The most significant of these are concerned with a world we cannot see, which even scientists cannot see, and which can only be proved by experiment: the world of sub-atomics.

You, me, and everything around us is made up of atoms; the chair you sit on, buildings, machinery, every animate and inanimate object in the visible world is composed of collections of atoms in continual movement which give an *impression* of solidity. But nothing is as it seems, for just as the universe is composed of 99% invisible matter, there is the great paradox that matter itself is just a manifestation of invisible energy, and *everything* in our 15,000-million year-old universe has its origin in that invisible force.

The entire physical world is held together by electromagnetism which stops us (and everything else) from falling to bits, and by gravity which prevents us from being thrown off the earth and into space. Christians see those facts as being in absolute conformity with the belief that our very being depends on God's will, and should he decide to suspend the scientific laws that maintain our existence, we would all simply vanish without trace – a sobering thought; and one cannot help being a little worried about the outcome if we ourselves go just one step too far in our assaults against the basic laws of nature and also of morality (increasingly the two are impinging on each other) which when violated contain their own punishment.

Just recently, an interesting hypothesis was put forward by an astronomer who suggested that our two closest planetary neighbours, Venus and Mars, may be a grim before-and-after picture of what conditions were like on Earth before life-forms evolved, and how it could *become* if we continue to destroy our ozone layer. He pointed out that Venus, gleaming with such beauty in the night sky, is in fact the nightmare reality of irreversible greenhouse effects, resulting in sulphuric acid rain from poisonous clouds of carbon dioxide. Above these clouds, temperatures rage at about 220°C, and below them just over 13°C. As for the daytime sky, Venus is a world without the colour blue; just an oppressive, monotonous orange. This completely uninhabitable planet (apart from any as-yet-undetectable lifeforms able to live in such an atmosphere) could, the astronomer pointed out, represent the initial conditions on Earth until it settled down into its present form.

Mars, on the other hand, with its thin carbon dioxide atmosphere, weak gravity, pink sky and lifeless landscape, could be what we are heading for unless we cherish our own precious ozone layer by single-mindedly protecting the environment. It is sobering to apply this before-and-after picture to our own Earth.

Stardust

Astronomers say that at least a billion Earth-like planets exist in the Milky Way, and that one star system 51 light years away – about 300 million million miles – might well contain life. Well, we may or may not find proof of this some time in the far-distant future, but what is not open to conjecture is that our relationship with the stars is closer than our ancestors could ever have imagined, for until the sixteenth century many people thought that everything in space was made of a single substance, ether, and that different consistencies were explained by the different densities of ether. But now we know that the elements from which stars are made are exactly the same elements from which we are made; every atom in our bodies was once part of a star. So tickled was I about this extraordinary fact that some years ago I felt inspired to adapt a well-known nursery rhyme to the subject.

> Twinkle, twinkle little star
> I don't wonder what you are
> Up above the world so high
> Made of the same stuff as I.

This was put in a more expert way during one of the most exhilarating events of 2003, the Royal Institution's

Christmas Lectures presented by Dr Monica Grady, Curator, Meteorite Collection and Head of Petrology Meteoritics at the Natural History Museum. The series of five lecture/demonstrations on Space and Time were watched by an audience of over 300 young boys and girls, and a million television viewers. Dr Grady's enthusiasm for her subject was reflected in the enthralled expression of the youngsters, and I wondered how many of them, inspired by what they heard and watched in the exciting demonstrations, may become our future astro-physicists or astronauts. Dr Grady explained that hydrogen (with some helium) was produced in the Big Bang: but all other elements have been produced since then in different types of stars, including supernovae, and without cycles of star birth and death, no carbon, or iron, or phosphorus, or any other element would have been formed. And without these elements, neither planets nor life would be possible. 'It is perhaps not always appreciated,' she said, 'that we are all, quite literally, made of stardust.'

Explanation for absolutely everything

Science is part of God's revelation; an invitation to learn, to discover how the world is made and how it functions. It is like a divine game invented for our enlightenment, excitement and even entertainment. So how dull and false is the premise that there is 'conflict' between religious faith and scientific facts, when these are just two sides of the same divine coin.

At present the scientific community continues its determined search to discover an elusive equation which they hope will unite all the major concepts in physics. Many of them believe that this unified theory will not only reveal once and for all the mysteries of how the universe operates, but also make belief in a personal Creator obsolete. Odd how it doesn't seem to occur to them that, even if and when they prove a unified theory, it will still not answer the real question: how did the universe come about?

For those who say they only believe in what they can see

or touch or prove for themselves, it is infuriating when others state that it was God who created scientific laws in the first place. But for believers it is simply a confirmation of the Credo, 'I believe in God the Father Almighty, maker of heaven and earth, and of all things *visible and invisible*'. St John of the Cross emphasized the profundity of this prayer when he wrote in his Spiritual Canticle, 'The invisible things of God are made known to the soul by created things, visible and invisible.' God respects our intelligence, but also expects us to use it to look and think and meditate beyond the appearance of things.

The mysteries of creation on all levels are being revealed step by step, at just the right rate to protect us from shock when faced with the limitless complexities of the cosmos, at a steady progression we take for granted. Perhaps it is no coincidence that so often scientists in different parts of the world come up with new discoveries at the same time. I use the word 'discoveries' because the fact is that scientists can never really create anything; they can only describe what is already there, and it took a Creator to put something there in the first place, because nothing can come from nothing. The crucial issue for the scientist is what use technology will make of the discovery, and whether it will be for the good or ill of humanity. In science, more than in any other discipline, the question of faith in God is not an academic one, for we all depend on those who work on the far frontiers of research and development that affect every aspect of our lives.

True enough, scientific research is always many years in advance of what we, the poor ignorant public, are told about it. But even the most brilliant scientists share one crucial drawback with us: they have a limited number of years on earth, confined to their own position in time and space; only God is outside these limitations. 'I am Alpha, I am Omega, the beginning of all things and their end.' And if the significance of that passage from the Book of Revelation is not sufficient to clarify the nature of God, we have the awesome and authoritative words of Jesus: 'Truly, truly, I say to you, before Abraham was, I am.'

Right now, some scientists are prematurely gleeful about their new best friend: chaos theory, which demonstrates that the sub-atomic world, at certain levels, does not follow a logical pattern and therefore cannot be predicted. 'You see!' is their triumphant reaction. 'That proves there is no orderly mind in charge of the universe. It's all down to chance.' Yet even as I write these words, a more enlightened scientist has said, 'Chaos can be misinterpreted, for it is really about hidden patterns'.

Even more significant for Christians is an aspect of modern physics which in an as yet puzzling way seems to indicate that the outcome of some experiments are directly affected by the person conducting the experiment, so that, incredibly, what we are and what we do, interacts with invisible sub-atomic particles of energy. Difficult as it is for us ordinary lay people to grasp the full significance of this, it is worth thinking about because the implications are mind-blowing.

A good question

What, you may ask, has all this to do with prayer? The answer is, everything, for when we pray we transcend our own space and time and enter into a new dimension that links us with God, and there are striking parallels between the invisible world of sub-atomic physics and the interplay between the human being and God during the real but invisible activity we call prayer, an activity which gives us the opportunity to apply order to chaos.

To extend the parallel even further: when we pray we are interacting with the Holy Spirit, and our prayers – if they are worthy and pleasing to God – can, and do, directly affect the outcome of what we are praying for. It can be compared with the physicists' famous 'butterfly effect', which says that the mere gentle flapping of butterfly wings at one end of the earth can set off a series of reactions in the natural world that could result in a hurricane thousands of miles away at the other end. In a similar way, if we pray humbly and sincerely, our prayers can result in a series of reactions on the spiritual plane that, figuratively (perhaps even literally, who knows?) can move mountains, just as in a profoundly personal way it changes the person who does the praying. Christ is our spiritual unified field, the complete answer to the deepest probings of the human soul.

Happily, one of the more encouraging signs of the times is the growing number of scientists who are prepared to stick their heads above the parapet and declare their belief in a God-driven universe. Russell Stannard is one of these. Professor Emeritus of Physics at the Open University, practising Christian and writer of best-selling books on science for youngsters, he was asked during a radio broadcast whether he really believed that God created the world. 'Yes, very much so,' he said. 'Science can demonstrate how the world developed but it cannot explain *why* it developed. Why there is something rather than nothing. That is not a scientific question, it is beyond the remit of science.'

On the location of heaven, he said,

> Space is really just an appearance. What is real is our four-dimensional reality. It has taken a long time to recognise that time is a kind of space, and space a kind of time – that's because we experience the two in such different ways and it's difficult to think of them as somehow being the same. But once you are forced to accept that as a scientist – and it's the only way to make sense of laboratory observations – you begin to think 'Is there a fifth dimension that we experience in some other way, and a sixth and a seventh, and so on?

This raises the possibility of heaven, purgatory and hell existing in different dimensions – a proposition likely to enrage atheist scientists, about whom Professor Stannard says:

> While most lay people are extremely reticent about speaking on scientific matters if they have no scientific training, there are some very famous scientists who, theologically speaking, have not got as far as Sunday School when it comes to discussing God, but they are quite happy to sound off on theological

matters despite the fact that their theology is that of a ten-year-old; but *because* they are famous, the public tend to take everything they say as being true, giving far more weight to their theological pronouncements than they deserve.

By contrast, one of this country's most respected scientists, Professor John Polkinghorne, former Professor of Mathematical Physics at Cambridge, Fellow of the Royal Society, is also an Anglican priest, whose writings on the science–theology debate continue to broaden the minds and deepen the understanding of God as only-begetter of science as well as of everything else.

During a lecture he gave at Wells Cathedral in 1993, Professor Polkinghorne said, 'The search for understanding, which is natural to a scientist is, in the end, the search for God.' Commenting on this book, one reviewer very pertinently pondered: 'Can it be that religion and science are not what most people think they are, and that their perceived antipathy is neither necessary nor natural?'

The frequent claims by atheists, scientists and others, that science and a belief in God cannot coexist, and that anyway the Catholic Church has always been anti-science, does not stand up to close scrutiny. Their ill-informed allegations are usually based not on prejudice – though this may sometimes play a part – but on ignorance. When St Albert the Great, the brilliant thirteenth-century Dominican and teacher of St Thomas Aquinas, was declared a Doctor of the Church in 1931, it demonstrated that by honouring such a man, famous for his genius both as a scientist and as a Catholic theologian, the Church confirmed that science and religion are simply different aspects of one truth.

Among the many scientists in more modern times whose vocation for science went hand-in-hand with deep religious faith, there were:

• Johannes Reinke, an internationally-renowned German botanist, who lived from 1849 to 1931, and said, 'Unless we close our eyes for fear of seeing, we are obliged to recognise the existence of a creative power which governs nature and maintains its regular course. The more we try to understand the puzzles of nature, the more we are subjugated by the reflection of his Divinity.'

- Max Planck, the great German physicist, who is particularly relevant because he was the author of quantum theory, the very basis of modern physics. I imagine the fact that he was also a deeply devout Catholic is a fact that anti-God physicists either do not know or prefer to brush aside. In his work, *Paths of Physical Knowledge*, published in 1944, Planck expressed what is now rapidly emerging as the spirit of the age: the convergence of science and faith in God:

> Nowhere, however far our vision extends and whatever we look at, do we find any contradiction between religion and the experimental sciences. Rather, we observe absolute harmony on all points. Religion and science are in no way mutually exclusive as many of our contemporaries believe and fear; on the contrary, they are in agreement and complement each other. The most direct proof that they are not incompatible is a historically established fact: the greatest scholars of all times were imbued with deep religious feeling.

- The last – and most succinct – word on the matter goes to Albert Einstein: 'Religion without science is lame, science without religion is blind.'

What else is new?

Over the years, the famous astrophysicist Stephen Hawking has always made it clear in his best-selling books that he regards a personal God as surplus to requirements, and that all the mysteries of the universe will be solved once scientists reach the ultimate goal of a theory about everything, the Unified Theory. But recently there has been something of a seismic shift in his stance. According to a newspaper report, Professor Hawking has now admitted that a unified theory would never be found. To be absolutely sure I had understood him correctly, I was put in touch with a member of his team at Cambridge University, who dictated to me the following direct statement for publication:

> In the last 100 years we have made spectacular advances in our understanding of the universe. We now know the laws that govern what happens in all but the most extreme conditions, like the origins of the universe and black holes. Many people, myself included, had hoped that we would soon find the ultimate theory that would hold even in these situations, and could be written down in a finite number of pages. This would enable us to predict everything in the universe. We now have a strong candidate, called M Theory, for this ultimate theory.
>
> However, M Theory is not a single theory, but a whole collection of theories, that are all different approximations of the same theory. It does not seen possible to formulate the underlying theory directly, but only by a series of better and better approximations to it. So we will never reach the end of our quest for a complete understanding of the universe.
>
> In a way, I'm glad. Science after finding the ultimate theory would be like mountaineering after Everest. The human race needs an intellectual challenge. It must be boring to be God and have nothing left to discover.

There is a real and refreshing humility in Stephen Hawking's conclusions (although his last sentence indicates he still has some way to go to understanding the nature of God) and I asked his Cambridge colleague if he would kindly put the following question to him: did he totally discount the possibility that Unified Theory might be in the domain of God? But I was warned that Professor Hawking never answers questions about or discusses God. 'Please tell him that I am a persistent nagger,' I replied. A week later, I had a phone call from my Cambridge contact who said that, much to his surprise, Stephen Hawking had agreed to respond to my question; his response was brief, and in two parts. The first obviously referred to my suggestion that Unified Theory belonged in God's domain, and his reply was: 'That is not the same question as "Do you believe in God?".' Which rather puzzled me. But the second part of his answer was more significant than the famous scientist may have realized, for he said, 'I believe God does not interfere to break the laws of Physics.' This appears to imply that he has not absolutely discounted God as a reality. Who knows, perhaps this statement had a round of applause from all those past, famous scientists who love God and his works, and now live the exciting life of heaven.

I wonder if Professor Hawking is aware that his 'amazing new theory' described in his famous book *The Universe in a Nutshell* published in 1991, was in fact first revealed some seven centuries ago. This theory, according to Hawking, was that 'Originally the universe was no bigger than a pea, and existed in this tiny state for a fraction of a second before that big bang 12 billion years ago created time and space.' In 1373, the great English mystic, Dame Julian of Norwich, in *her* famous book, *Revelations of Divine Love*, wrote about one of her visions of Our Lord.

Using an analogy that pre-echoes the title of Stephen Hawking's book, Dame Julian wrote:

> He showed me a little thing, the size of a hazelnut, which seemed to lie in the palm of my hand; and it was as round as any ball. I looked upon it with the eye of my understanding, and thought, What may this be? I was answered in a general way, thus: 'It is all that is made'. I wondered how long it would last; for it seemed as though it might suddenly fade away to nothing, it was so small. And I was answered in my understanding: It lasts, and shall last; for God loveth it. And even so hath everything being by the love of God.

It is quite startling to learn that it has taken some seven hundred years for a modern scientist to produce information that Dame Julian received direct from God, and though it puzzled her at the time, is now accepted by the majority of physicists as the origin of the universe: a tiny ball of matter of incalculable density whose explosion resulted in the expanding universe in which we are all living. As Our Lord told her in 1373, 'It is all that is made.'

He also made it clear to Dame Julian that creation is an act of love. Christians, after all, are so used to saying that God is love; it is the basic tenet of our faith, but our insight into the profound meaning of this should deepen when we begin to understand that the Cosmos and all its contents are the result of an explosion of love, and that by a closer relationship with him through prayer we can tap into that love, and transform not just our lives, but also help to transform the world in which we live.

2

Inner Space

The French philosopher, Pascal, writing about our position in the universe, described human beings as being 'suspended between the two infinities, of immensity and vanishingly small'. So, switching our gaze from the immeasurable depths of the universe and the invisible world of sub-atomics, let us turn our attention to the immeasurable depths and invisible world of our secret interior life, to that inner space where the soul resides.

Earlier, we faced the startling fact that in the most literal sense we are children of the cosmos, variations on God's theme. It is only when we fully appreciate the link between each one of us and the universe itself, that we can take the first step towards a true understanding of prayer as we join God in his own milieu, outside space and time.

The implications of this are that our prayers can encompass past and future as well as the present. For instance, we have it within our spiritual power to pray for those who were martyred for the Faith in past centuries, so that their pain may have been lessened at the hour of the greatest suffering.

In the same way, we should also pray for those who will live in the future. We can pray for the Church of the future, for Christians of the future, for young members of our family and for those yet unborn, whom we may never live to see as adults. And in carrying out these acts of love (for prayer is essentially an act of love) we should most especially thank God for the use he will make of our prayers.

What exactly is prayer?

Well, a dictionary description defines it as 'praise', 'thanksgiving' and 'supplication'. But while these are all vital elements of prayer, the most important of all is 'worship', for our love to be joined with awe. Prayer is our permanent means of direct communication with God (reaching its pinnacle through the Holy Sacrifice of the Mass) and is not confined to moments of crisis when we are in desperate need of help, but should become a constant interior activity, an awareness of the invisible world of God where we join his angels and saints in thanking him for his creation.

Sometimes people ask bitterly, 'What do we have to thank God for, when so many terrible things are happening in the world – so much violence and injustice?' When there are train crashes, when buildings collapse, when murderers run amok and kill innocent victims, 'Where was God then?' grieving families will cry. And here we come to the fundamental nub of the matter: it is not God who should be blamed when such tragedies occur, but us humans who are guilty of personal wickedness in the case of murder and other forms of violence, and, in the case of often avoidable tragic accidents, guilty of faulty workmanship, poor maintenance, incompetence, laziness, stupidity or carelessness. Unfortunately, only too often those in authority refuse to accept responsibility for such disasters. Time and again, it is God who is blamed for the failings of human beings, as if he were some kind of puppet-master and we were marionettes, without free will, without immortal souls, without possibility of salvation: no heaven, purgatory or hell.

'But what about when people are killed in natural disasters such as avalanches or drowning or earthquakes. Who's responsible then?' people ask – a question which leads us into an aspect of Christianity that is rarely mentioned.

As Christians we know that spiritually we are all flawed human beings; baptism washes away the wound of original sin, but unless we are saints a scar remains which can only be healed after a stay in purgatory has made us suitable for heaven. But the damage of the Fall, that initial rebellion against God, extends far beyond ourselves, for it also affected the entire natural world, inserting a potential for hostility into the relationship between mankind and the rest of creation. Man fights back, taming or adapting to nature in dangerous environments, finding cures for lethal viruses and bacteria; but there is a limit, and not unless they have both been drugged will the lion lie down with the lamb – not in our world, not ever.

Only when we accept – often with reluctance – that we are all imperfect beings living in an imperfect though beautiful world where there is never going to be prolonged peace, and that humans will always have to deal with violence and injustice: only then will we fully understand that our purpose during our lives here on earth should be to use whatever talents, gifts or skills we have (and everyone has some talent, gift or skill) to improve the world in which we live. It is personal prayer that can elevate even the most modest talent into an offering to God on a par with the most brilliantly gifted, if it has been carried out to the best of one's ability and with love. Without this spiritual input, a man or woman may become famous, prosperous and honoured, but it is a chilling and observable fact that without prayer the soul shrivels, and when we neglect the spiritual umbilical cord through which God nourishes our spirit, a desensitization takes place which over time, diminishes our character and distances us from his grace.

Prayer as weapon

Prayer is not only our comfort and protection; it is also our weapon, supplying the means by which we can connect with all the power of heaven to help us fight the good fight against what may appear to be overwhelming evils.

Our feeling of helplessness in the face of increasing corruption in public life, moral squalor, the undermining of family values, assaults on the very concept of decent behaviour, can be converted into constructive dependence on God. Just as the winner in certain forms of unarmed combat triumphs not by superior physical strength but by using the momentum of his opponent's moves to overthrow him, so we can pray for Our Lady's intercession to help in her own way to overthrow wickedness.

God is our major and exclusive secret weapon which we know with absolute certainty that the wicked do not possess. This certainty is based on the theological fact that prayer is the direct result of the promptings of the Holy Spirit. True, there are people in the world who call on God as they kill or maim in his name, but that is not prayer; it is the wickedest kind of blasphemy, which they will have to answer for in due course when they find themselves in the presence of the One they have insulted. Meanwhile, we can pray for the conversion of souls, and for the emergence of more good, clever men and women to expose and fight against the bad influences harming human society.

Prayer connects us with the divine reality which, at present, we can only glimpse 'through a glass darkly', and whenever we pray we are contributing to the funds of a great spiritual capital that can be drawn upon by other Christians who will follow us in the future.

G. K. Chesterton wrote prophetically on this aspect of prayer: 'The modern world, with its modern movements, is living on its Catholic capital. It is using, and using up, the truths that remain to it out of the old treasury of Christendom.' His use of the word 'capital' referred specifically to the spiritual treasure of the Church that had accumulated in this country up to the Reformation, and if he were alive today perhaps Chesterton would find little difference between the various Christian denominations and those Catholic churches which appear to have fulfilled some of the aims of the sixteenth-century Reformers. Yet, as a great fighter for truth, he would no doubt find a certain mischievous glee at the prospect of a return to the catacombs – in spirit if not in fact – and would embark on his unique form of literary guerilla warfare against the wide spectrum of enemies – without and within – howling at the gates of Rome.

As Christians, our most urgent task now is to increase the spiritual capital that is running out so quickly and which can only be restored by massive injections of prayer and penance; if the first is sufficiently profound, the second will follow, and in this supernatural warfare, the religious contemplative orders are in the front line. Those communities of monks and nuns, quietly spending lives of prayer away from the public gaze, are essential to the well-being of the Mystical Body, for that permanent means of devotion to God provides the spiritual under-pinning of our society, for believer and non-believer alike. Those corporate and individual prayers are like a steady, perfectly-running engine that works so well and unobtrusively that we do not even notice it.

Typical are the Adorers of the Sacred Heart in central London. This contemplative Order, founded by a French-woman, Adèle Garnier, follows the Rule of St Benedict. Every twenty minutes, throughout night and day, the nuns take turns to pray before the Blessed Sacrament in the chapel, where many Londoners and visitors escape from the city's clamour outside to recharge their spiritual batteries. One becomes very aware in this chapel that this is where the real, significant action is taking place; not in the exterior noisy hub of the capital, but here in the silence, close to the spot where the English martyrs were murdered four centuries ago, and where spiritual capital is being built up day after day, year after year, century after century, for the salvation of the human race.

For our part, the contemplative communities deserve our gratitude for their invaluable contribution in the battle against the powers of darkness which encourage those trends that undermine human society in one way or another. Each succeeding generation has to deal with this. But there are reasons for hope because, though religious

vocations generally have fallen sharply in the past forty
years, there has been an astonishing increase in vocations
to the contemplative Orders. Could this be because in
some communities, both secular and religious, spirituality
has been replaced with an agenda of meetings, committees
and conferences, so that the deep need for a life of prayer,
felt by many men and women with religious vocations,
has been sidelined?

Prayer and self-discovery

One of the most striking characteristics of the age we live
in is the feverish search by so many people all over the
world for a personal spirituality. This growing phenome-
non has led to a return of paganism in the form of New
Age cults; guru-driven sects; a vast variety of isms and
osophies; a sudden stampede by show-biz stars and other
celebrities to the esoteric complexities of the ancient
Hebrew Kabbalah; and the invention of new names for old
Christian heresies (the dictionary meaning of this term is
straightforward enough: 'An option contrary to the orthodox tenets of a religious body').

All these contemporary movements, though differing in
rites and practices, share one thing in common: they are
centred on self rather than on God. Hunger for truth has
been replaced by hunger for pseudo-mysticism which
bypasses the realities of a living faith. As T. S. Eliot wrote
in one of his poems: 'They constantly try to escape from
darkness outside and within by dreaming of systems so
perfect that no one will need to be good. But the man that
is will shadow the man that pretends to be.'

How frequently we read about well-known people
announcing they are taking time off to 'get in touch' with
themselves, to 'search' for themselves. But instead of
praying for truth, they play with crystals, toy with spiritu-
alism rather than spirituality, and experiment with drugs
– that soul-destroying cul-de-sac from which permanent
escape is rare.

Yet there is a simple and wholly effective way for

people to 'find' themselves; it never fails but it does involve pain.

The first step to genuine self-knowledge is to place ourselves humbly into God's hands and pray, very simply, for truth. It may take years, but gradually, through this sincere prayer and the circumstances of our lives, the interior self-protective skins of our being are stripped off layer by layer, revealing to us the truth about ourselves. Sometimes our hearts need to be broken before God can heal us and make us whole, a process involving agonizing remorse for the harm we have done to others through hard words, cruel actions, selfishness, or worse. Perhaps that is the purpose of purgatory, a healing dimension that makes us worthy of heaven by giving us the opportunity to complete our remorse for wrongs we have done but forgotten about. There is no opportunity for remorse in hell.

Meanwhile, new young souls, children, whose natural curiosity and sense of wonder about the world are so full of potential, are being side-tracked by irresponsible adults into questionable pastimes that have inherent dangers. For instance, some foolish people in the field of psychology have claimed that witchcraft is a form of spiritual activity. They do not mention the fact that to encourage youngsters to dabble in such puerile practices could lead the more impressionable among them to believe they have super-natural powers.

A few years ago in Mexico, an enthusiast of the Aztec and Inca civilizations asked a local Mexican Indian why he had become a Catholic. The Indian replied, 'Because in all our ancient religions the people were sacrificed to the God: Christianity is the only religion where God sacrificed himself for the people.'

Ways of praying

Prayer is the fundamental characteristic of Christian life. If you do not pray, you are not a Christian: it is as simple as that. There are times when we pray without enthusiasm, in exhaustion or depression, but our feelings or moods are irrelevant; the saints understood this and have said that prayer from a dry heart or mind, where every thought has to be dredged out of our own tiredness or apathy, is often the most valuable kind of prayer because it is the result of our will, and not of how we happen to feel at the moment. However, we must use common sense too. The great Spanish mystic, St Teresa of Avila, once arrived at a Carmelite convent and found that an excess of mortification had resulted in nervous tension among the community there. So what did she instruct her nuns to do? More prayer? More penance? More fasting? No, she wisely told them to get an extra hour's sleep. When we are exhausted or ill, or under severe stress, we should keep things simple, commending ourselves to God with a brief loving prayer.

Essential basis for prayer

The one absolute interior condition for prayer is humility. Without this, we may as well give up before we begin. Our Lord made it quite clear: 'Unless you be as little children ...' Not childish, but childlike, recognizing what we are and what he is. That is the secret of praying properly: to understand, acknowledge and accept that in his eyes we are little children, created beings with limited lifespans, although we sometimes behave as if we were the lords and masters of creation. We need to think deeply about the awesomeness of this fact every time we approach God in prayer.

In fact, if I were asked to sum up the two greatest evils in the world, I would suggest they are lack of humility, and greed, for from these two failings grow most other evils. But let us be clear about the meaning of humility. It does *not* mean a kind of cringing meekness, but rather a sense of reality about what we are and who God is – the Being who created us and everything else. It is no good giving lip-service to this basic truth; we should absorb its implication into our souls. He loves us with a love so overwhelming that over two thousand years ago he entered our space-time continuum as the Second Person of the Holy Trinity in order to die for us. The Creator of the cosmos humbled himself to that unimaginable extent; his humility was essential for our salvation.

Prayer as subversion

I once mentioned to a nun that when I travelled on the London Underground I always prayed for everyone on the train. 'Which line?' she asked. 'The Bakerloo,' I said. She laughed; 'I do the same on the Circle and Metropolitan lines.' It makes me wonder just how many Christians are showering the British – or any other of the world's transport systems – with silent prayers. Quite a large number, I would guess, for the invisible and secret world of interior prayer gives us immense power to do good to people we come across in the comings and goings of our daily lives. We can pray for the salvation and well-being of those who have no idea what we are up to. Men and women who may look sad, ill, angry, neglected – we can scatter prayers left, right and centre, asking God to help them. And when we listen to or read about people attacking Christianity, we can pray for the sweet revenge of their conversion.

There are many types of prayer, but this book is based on a method that has as its inspiration Luke 2:19, when, following the shepherds' visit to the Infant Jesus in the manger 'Mary kept all these things, pondering them in her heart'. And again, in Luke 2:51, after her young Son had been found at the Temple in Jerusalem, 'His mother kept all these things in her heart'.

When momentous events or experiences happen to us in the course of our lives it is often only years later that we fully understand the effect they have had on us. From the moment that Mary was told by the Angel Gabriel that she had been chosen to bear our Saviour, her destiny was fixed: she was unique. But few people at the time knew who she really was as she dedicated her entire life to loving and bringing up her beloved Son.

During all those years she watched the baby grow into a child, then from a boy into a young man, and then to a mature adult, with the growing realization of his true nature in her innermost thoughts. The joys, the sorrows, the public life and the final glories, were all thought about, pondered in Mary's heart. That is what Christian contemplation or meditation means: pondering, thinking about God. And in this book we follow Mary's way, and meditate on the events of her Son's life by means of that special form of prayer the world knows as the Rosary.

PART II

THE ROSARY SPECIFICALLY

3

About the Rosary

Moving from the ever-unfolding mysteries of outer space to the invisible mysteries of inner space, we reach our final destination: the specific yet transcendent mysteries of the Rosary.

What makes the Rosary so special? Why is this seemingly simple system of prayer considered to be the most important spiritual aid to salvation after the Mass? Why as recently as the year 2002, did John Paul II issue an Apostolic Letter, *Rosarium Virginis Mariae*, calling for the Rosary to be rediscovered?

Origins of the Rosary

There are numerous, detailed books about the Rosary's origins, so we know that beads have been used as a way to count prayers by many religions. We also know they were used by Catholics to count devotional prayers to Jesus and Mary in the thirteenth century. But this method of prayer developed slowly over time, and it was not until the fifteenth century that the form and content of the devotion were finally organized by a Dominican friar, Alain de la Roche, and named the Dominican Rosary.

What then of the tradition that Our Lady appeared to St Dominic and promised him success in his preaching against the Albigensian heresy if he used the Rosary which she gave to him? Well, curiously enough, the origin of this story has been traced back to none other than Alain de la Roche himself, describing an event he alleged had happened two centuries earlier, but for which – the Dominican Order points out – there is no proof or evidence of any kind.

St Dominic fought vigorously against the Albigensian heresy, his weapons being prayer, and his powerful preaching. The Albigensians believed that God's power was limited to the spiritual world, and that the material world was ruled by Satan.

They had no Mass because they did not believe in the Blessed Sacrament, indeed they did not believe in any of the sacraments, nor did they have any churches; all this, as well as their denial of Jesus, contempt for marriage and consequent abandonment to the extremes of licentiousness, were just a few characteristics of their descent into a spiritual wasteland. To counter this attack on Christianity, the right man appeared at the right time: St Dominic. Because the basis of Dominican spirituality is love for the incarnation, St Dominic's newly-founded Order of Preachers was the ideal antidote to this particular heresy. The Dominicans abhor any belief which despises the material world, for in Genesis 1:31 God called his work 'Very good'; God loves and blesses the world he made and Dominicans rejoice at God's becoming flesh and dwelling among us; they also have a great devotion to his greatest creation, Our Lady.

Yet while St Dominic may well have used beads to count the psalms and popular prayers of the time to Christ and Our Lady, they were not in the form of the Rosary as we know it. And nowhere in the early biographies of St Dominic, in his sermons, in the historical chronicles of the Dominican Order, and most significantly, in the acts of his canonization, is there any mention of the Rosary; nor is he depicted holding, or in the proximity of, a Rosary in any of the religious art of the period. The understanding is that Alain de la Roche simply followed a custom of the time: that of crediting a famous name with an enterprise in order to ensure its success; according to the *New Catholic Dictionary* this 'was regarded as a quite normal means of religious propaganda in Alain's period'.

This early example of successful public relations certainly makes good sense when we learn that apart from organizing the final form of the Rosary, Alain was also one of the founders and popularizers of the Rosary Confraternity which ever since has spread the devotion and become a worldwide movement that continues under the auspices of the Dominicans. What is beyond any doubt is that the Rosary has always been, and continues to be, the greatest treasure of the Dominican Order, and its spiritual gift to the entire Christian world.

The Rosary and Scripture

Both in his preaching and writings, St Dominic encouraged the study of the Old and the New Testaments, and a member of the Order recently emphasized to me how significant it is that John Paul II is taking the Rosary into a new stage and tying it into the New Testament, affirming the Second Vatican Council's Dogmatic Constitution on Revelation, *Dei Verbum*, which includes the affirmation of St Jerome in Chapter 6 of his *Commentary on Isaiah*, that 'ignorance of scripture is ignorance of Christ'. This is strongly supported by John Paul II in *Rosarium Virginis Mariae*, where on the indispensable role of Scripture in praying the Rosary, he says:

> I also place my trust in you, theologians: by your sage and rigorous reflection, rooted in the word of God and sensitive to the lived experience of the Christian people, may you help them to discover the Biblical foundations, the spiritual riches and the pastoral value of this traditional prayer.

I have found (and have learned that many other people have found), and I highly recommend, the practice of having a New Testament at hand, to read the relevant chapters in the Gospels and Acts 1, before praying each decade of the Rosary. This is a truly thrilling experience, because it brings the various Mysteries into vivid life, and prepares the ground for the meditation that follows.

Though this is not always possible if you are praying the Rosary away from home, you will find that once you get used to reading them, the Gospel events will become so clear in your mind, that you will eventually find yourself recalling them without having to look up the scriptural references.

In fact, it was the New Testament that started my unexpected journey into the Catholic Church. As a Jewess, I had never even looked at it before; it was forbidden territory, and when I eventually did, it was in response to a challenge. I was with some friends who had brought along a young actor about to leave the stage to enter a seminary. While he was talking to the others about becoming a priest, I kept making anti-Christian remarks, until he suddenly asked me if I had ever read the New Testament. 'Certainly not!' I replied. 'Well, then,' he said, 'before you start attacking Christianity, at least have the courtesy to find out what you're talking about.' Chastened, I got hold of a New Testament, sat down and read it from beginning to end. It turned my world upside down. In brief, by the last page I had emerged a different person from the one who had opened the first page. So it has often astonished me since then to discover how few Catholics have actually *read* the New Testament rather than dipping into it occasionally, or listening to the gospel readings at Mass.

The Holy Father describes the Rosary as a 'Compendium of the Gospel' and says, 'How many graces I have received in these years from the Blessed Virgin Mary from the Rosary', and then reminds us that when Pope Leo XIII promulgated his own Rosary encyclical, he recommended it as 'an effective weapon against the ills afflicting society'. Few would disagree that such a weapon is even more urgently needed in our own society. Referring to his decree again, the Pope sets the record straight about a misunderstanding that has caused much disquiet among those who have not read the conciliar documents.

The timeliness of this proposal is evident from a number of considerations. First the urgent need to counter a certain crisis of the Rosary, which in the present historical and theological context can risk being wrongly devalued, and therefore no longer taught to the younger generation. There are some who think the centrality of the Liturgy stressed by the Second Vatican Ecumenical Council necessarily entails giving lesser importance to the Rosary. Yet, as Pope Paul VI made clear, not only does this prayer not conflict with the Liturgy, *it sustains it*, since it serves as an excellent introduction and faithful echo of the Liturgy, enabling people to participate fully and interiorly in it and to reap its fruit in their daily lives.

Ways of praying the Rosary

When we pray the Rosary we are placing ourselves at Mary's side as she leads us to ponder, to meditate, on the major events of Our Lord's life, death, and resurrection. It is not an occasion for speed but for reflection, and in various apparitions Mary has said that it is better to pray one decade slowly and thoughtfully, rather than to rush through it. In the privacy of our home we can set our own pace, but often in church when people are praying the Rosary in a group, large or small, the words sound garbled because some people are praying faster and some slower than others, without any attempt at synchronization, so it all becomes more of a penance than an act of devotion. Nor, in my experience do those who are leading the Rosary – priests or laity – mention that a steady, slow rhythm, clearly spoken by all should be an obligatory courtesy to Mary. It would of course take more time, but even if only two or three decades could be prayed in this way, at least it would be more in the reflective spirit of the devotion.

From time to time, people have asked me whether they should meditate before or during the saying of the prayers. This is really a matter of personal preference. There is a school of thought which believes that the meditation should form a background to the prayers, and that it doesn't matter about the words as long as the person saying them is recollected and praying with concentration.

Another view is that the meditation comes first, followed by the prayers, every word of each decade to be prayed slowly with due awareness that they are being addressed to our Father and to Mary. I doubt that I am the only person whose favourite place to pray the Rosary is alone, in church, in front of the Blessed Sacrament.

There are varying customs about the beginning and end of each Rosary, as certain prayers have been added over the years. For instance, many people start by praying the Our Father on the first bead, followed by three Hail Marys and a Glory Be on the last bead, before embarking on the Mysteries, and they often complete each decade with the Fatima prayer, 'O my Jesus, forgive us our sins ...'. Like many other Catholics, though, I am inclined to follow the simpler Dominican method: to begin without any preliminaries, and to end with the Hail Holy Queen. As one priest, Fr Jerome Pokorny has said, 'The Rosary is like a chain tying time to eternity.'

Many people keep a little one-decade chain in their pocket or handbag which they can use during their day to cast prayers around wherever they happen to be, and whenever an intention springs to mind. I've often thought that if the trajectory of these prayers could be traced as a series of dots or lines on a computer screen, in the way the movements of people walking around cities has sometimes been shown, it would probably astonish everyone to see how much secret prayer is being spread around in daily life.

We don't even need beads. We have ten fingers. When the tragic Hungarian martyr, Cardinal Mindszenty, was being tortured by the Communists who had taken over his country, he continued to pray the Rosary; in his own words, 'With my fingers I tried to pray the Rosary ... I said the Rosary on my fingers.'

High on a hill above Barcelona, local people and visitors enjoy strolling around a delightful spot called Guëll Park, designed by the famous Catalan architect, a deeply devout Catholic, Antonio Gaudí. Walking along the main pathway, those with observant eyes will notice a series of white-painted rocks placed at regular intervals, each representing a bead of the Rosary, so that anyone wishing to pray it can do so interiorly, during the walk.

It is easy to be misled by the Rosary's apparent simplicity, yet it has been prayed and recommended by the most profound mystics and countless saints, for within itself it contains reverence, worship, love for and confidence in God, and Our Lady's power to intercede for us; it places those who pray it on the same level. Riches, power, intellect, station in life, educational background, are irrelevant, for when we pray the Rosary, we all start at the same point: humility before and utter dependence on God. For evidence of this, we only need to take a quick look at some of the people throughout history who have loved this prayer:

- Bernadette at Lourdes, who described seeing Mary holding a Rosary
- the little shepherd children, Francisco, Jacinta and Lucia, at Fatima where in 1917 Mary introduced herself to them as the Lady of the Rosary (and also prophesied the Second World War and the rise of Communism)
- St Francis de Sales
- St Alphonsus Liguori who said, 'My eternal salvation depends on saying the Rosary'
- St Louis Marie de Montfort
- St Padre Pio
- St John Bosco, who in his dream prophesied the winning of the battle of Lepanto and the saving of Christian civilization by the intervention of Our Lady obtained through the prayers of the Rosary
- famous scientists and artists, including Louis Pasteur, Michelangelo, Mozart, Haydn, and Gluck.

Then there are the popes, men often surrounded by the ceremonial and panoply of the Vatican, but whose spirituality was centred on the Mass first and then the Rosary:

- Boniface VIII
- Clement V
- Clement VII, who wrote nineteen encyclicals on the Rosary
- Gregory XVI
- Pius IX
- Leo XIII
- Pius XII
- John XXIII
- Paul VI
- John Paul I
- – up to the present with our Holy Father John Paul II, whose love of the Rosary permeates every word of his numerous Marian writings.

If such a variety of people, from the poorest to the richest, from the illiterate to those of towering intellect and power, with little else in common except their shared humanity, if they discovered, and their successors still discover, something unique in the Rosary, then surely it cannot be ignored.

There is only one occasion when we should *not* be praying the Rosary, and that is during Mass, when all our attention and concentration should be directed at the actions of the priest who is offering up the Blessed Sacrament as a Holy Sacrifice for our sins. At that moment, nothing else matters, though, of course, we can pray the Rosary in thanksgiving after Mass.

Finally, we should not hesitate to offer up our Rosary prayers for our specific intentions. God longs for us to turn to him for our needs and to ask his Mother for her powerful intercession on our behalf. The moment we pray to Christ we are demonstrating our belief, and that is all it takes to nurture our relationship with him. He will help in every aspect of our lives, but we have to ask him first. If we sometimes think that some of our prayers must seem very trivial to God, that is because we still do not fully understand that he truly *is* our Father, and what father does not respond to his children's hurts or needs? By giving his Mother to us as our maternal protector, we know that Mary will present our requests, our sorrows, our joys, to Jesus. They are interested in every detail of our lives, as we are of those we love.

In our times, just reading the newspapers, listening to the radio or watching television, is enough to plunge us into sadness, rage and frustration at our apparent inability to do anything about abuse of power, neglect of the vulnerable, violence, corruption, terrorism (increasingly directed at Christian communities), and the inherent dangers in a society that ignores Christ. But we should take heart, for we really can fight back by converting the energy, which we are wasting in angry despair, into a spiritual force through the Rosary. By means of it we can offer up our specific intentions to Our Lady after each of the Mysteries, asking for her help not just in our personal worries but for solutions to those specific problems and situations that are frightening and angering all people of goodwill in our time. And it is always a great act of love to offer Mary a decade for someone, somewhere, whom *we* don't know but Mary does, and who may be in great need of our prayers.

As Christians, it is important for us to accept that we are not only living in an era when there are savage wars in so many parts of the world, but that there is also a real spiritual war taking place, and never have the prayers of the Rosary been more urgently needed. Believe me, it works: not always immediately, but in God's own time and his own way.

In the Introduction, I said that I would explain how I came to pray the Rosary regularly rather than spasmodically. It was during the years when I was living and working in Spain. One day, during lunchtime, a journalist friend came rushing over to me in a state of great agitation. 'Ruth, come quickly!' he said. 'There's been a major disaster up the road, the Hotel Costa has collapsed and two little English children are buried under the rubble – the parents need someone English to be with them.' We both rushed to the scene, which was horrific. All the emergency services were there, ambulances, fire engines, police cars, everyone looking helplessly at the mountains of concrete and plaster, bricks and steel, that completely covered the scene. It seemed impossible that anyone could have survived. The parents were a piteous sight. The white-faced father, in shock, couldn't utter a word, while the distraught mother sobbed over and over again, 'My little boys, they're inside, my little boys are dead inside.' I made the usual soothing sounds, but my heart sank as I had been told by the men who had been trying to get through the rubble that there was no possibility at all that the two children, one three years old, the other five, could still be alive. The hotel, a fairly new one (I have changed the name) had its swimming pool built on the roof, which had collapsed, bringing down the whole building.

More than two hours went by, while men from the various emergency services tried fruitlessly to get through the rubble, when suddenly another friend of mine, Enrique, a well-known figure in the local tourism industry, suddenly grabbed a hard hat, and said he was determined to go in. Onlookers tried to stop him, as they were afraid he would bring more rubble down on himself. But he ignored their advice, and somehow pushed his way through all the ruins. The children's mother said to me, 'At least let them try to get their little bodies out. They can't just leave them there.'

Like everyone else, I felt utterly useless in such a situation, but desperately I prayed to Our Lady and made a promise to pray the Rosary every day for two years if the children survived. (Please note the limitation of time: not very worthy, but being realistic about myself, I knew that I was more likely to stick to my promise for that length of time, rather than – as a more saintly person would have done – making a lifelong promise.)

Some twenty minutes later, we heard faint shouting from beneath the rubble. It became louder, and a cheer came up from the onlookers gathered around the spot where Enrique had managed to find a way through. Eventually, we could all hear him clearly. 'It's all right,' he shouted, 'I found them. They're alive!' A steel beam had fallen in such a way as to protect them from the collapsing building all around them. When I gave the wonderful news to the parents they couldn't believe it, and cried with joy. The next day, it made front-page news in the newspapers, which reported, 'Not only were the children found alive, but neither of them had a scratch or bruise on them. The only way to describe what happened is to say it was truly a miracle.'

With Our Lady anything is possible.

4

The Five Joyful Mysteries

First Joyful Mystery

The Annunciation

In the sixth month the angel Gabriel was sent from God to a city of Galilee named Nazareth, to a virgin betrothed to a man whose name was Joseph, of the house of David; and the virgin's name was Mary. And he came to her and said, 'Hail, full of grace, the Lord is with you!'. But she was greatly troubled at the saying, and considered in her mind what sort of greeting this might be. And the angel said to her, 'Do not be afraid, Mary, for you have found favour with God. And behold, you will conceive in your womb and bear a son, and you shall call his name Jesus. He will be great and will be called the Son of the Most High; and the Lord God will give to him the throne of his father David, and he will reign over the house of Jacob for ever; and of his kingdom there will be no end.'

Luke 1:26–35

One of the first questions to arise in many minds is, Why did God choose this particular young woman at that particular time in the history of the world? Why not earlier on? Or for that matter, why not much later, closer to what we think of as modern times? But isn't the very term 'modern' meaningless? Doesn't each generation consider itself modern? At this very instant (and what could be more modern than that?) you, I and everyone else are creating a past for future generations.

The fact remains that for reasons beyond our earthly

knowledge, the specific moment selected by God for the Annunciation was unique; some divine conjunction of circumstances on Earth, perhaps in the universe, had co-incided to present the right person at the right moment in space and time: Mary in Nazareth.

Luke says that Mary was 'greatly troubled' by the angel Gabriel's greeting. I would guess that 'troubled' is putting it mildly, yet she pushed all misgivings aside and unhesi-tatingly accepted her key role in our salvation when she responded with the beautiful words: 'Behold, I am the handmaid of the Lord; let it be to me according to your word' (Luke 1:38).

Mary's childhood
As we are told so little about Our Lady's family, we can only speculate about their circumstances, but tradition has it that Mary's childhood was spent in Sepphoris, the then flour-ishing capital of Galilee, only five miles from Nazareth.

Greek in origin, Sepphoris was a finely laid-out city with a large population, military garrisons and a busy hub for commerce, where people would come from all around the region to do their shopping. It was also famous as a centre for Talmudic learning. Joachim, Hannah and Miriam (to give Anna and Mary their real Hebrew names) would have been familiar with the civic centre at the top of the hill and its panoramic view of the beautiful surrounding countryside, where today visitors can look down to the modest Catholic church named after Our Lady's parents.

Although it is unlikely that Anna and Joachim were wealthy, it is also unlikely that they were peasants as sometimes depicted, for their family was of sufficient status to have a cousin – Zechariah – who was a Temple priest. All Jews were expected to be able to read and write, to know the Bible more or less by heart, and to possess similar familiarity with the Talmud, and, as we shall see in the next chapter, Mary's own profound knowledge of Holy Scriptures was evident in the way she responded to Elizabeth's greeting at the Visitation.

What did Our Lady look like?
Often, in some religious paintings, Mary is pictured according to the nationality of the artist: Anglo-Saxon, Mediterranean, Nordic, Indian, Japanese, Latin-American, among others. Only rarely do they reflect the most likely appearance of Our Lady during her life on earth: a young Middle Eastern Jewess with the dark eyes and hair of her race and region. Whether their hair was straight or curly, unmarried Jewesses wore it long, and often loose. But once they were married, convention dictated that it was immodest for married women to be seen in public with loose hair and their heads uncovered. So after her marriage, Mary's hair would have probably been coiled behind her head, perhaps plaited or braided; only at home would it have been unfastened and left loose.

Home life
Only wealthy people could afford spacious houses, usually built of locally quarried stone and with lavish decorations. Most Jewish people, however, lived in traditional two-storey houses, mostly made of clay bricks, which were mixed with straw and baked in an oven. The ground floor would have been used for household equipment, storage and even for some domestic animals, and it also came in handy as a children's play area. On a higher level there would be a room or a number of rooms, depending on the economic status of the family. Many homes had wooden beds (and once Joseph was a member of the family, he probably found himself in demand for carpentry services to his in-laws and other new relatives). Some people used sleeping mats or bedrolls, often filled with wool. Covering was provided by hand-woven quilts; others were made of goat hair; during the day these would be rolled up and put in a corner out of the way.

One of the most important parts of any house (and this continues today in many Middle Eastern countries) was the flat roof; this was used for outdoor sleeping during very hot weather, and as a general recreation area where parents, children, grandparents and the rest of the family could get together. Friends and neighbours would join them for this rooftop social life, which encouraged a close community spirit, especially as the houses were built so close to each other – sometimes just a few inches apart – that neighbours could easily step from one roof to another. By law there had to be a surrounding wall, about a metre high, to protect people, especially children, from toppling over. This touchingly practical aspect of Jewish architecture goes back to the time of Moses (Deuteronomy 22:8) who, explaining the laws of God, said: 'When you build a new house, you shall make a parapet for your roof, that you may not bring the guilt of blood upon your house, if anyone fall from it.' The roof also had a slight slope to ensure that rain would be carried down to the gutters.

But whether the owners were rich or poor, the front door of every Jewish home had a mezuzah attached to it; this is a tiny scroll of paper bearing a Hebrew phrase passed on by Moses: 'You shall write them on the door-posts of your house', were God's instructions. And on the back of the parchment was written the Hebrew word for 'Almighty', together with the initial Hebrew letters for the phrase, 'Guardian of the doors of Israel'. This was then rolled up and inserted into a narrow tube about three to four inches long with a tiny aperture through which that word was visible, and it was then fixed, slanting inwards, on to the doorpost.

As this ancient custom of invoking God's blessing on the home began around the time of the building of Herod's temple, it is quite certain that not only Our Lady's parents, but also Mary and Joseph's house would have had mezuzahs in place and, as anyone who has visited a Jewish home may have observed, this custom continues to the present day.

What sort of clothes would the Holy Family have worn?
It's surprising how many people, if you pin them down, don't actually understand why the Jews are known as God's 'chosen people'. This term is sometimes resented by others who feel that somehow the Jews have staked a

personal claim on God; but it was God who staked a claim on them, for they were unique in their worship of one God as supreme spirit and creator – a belief embodied in their two ancient prayers: 'Hear O Israel, the Lord is God, the Lord is One', and 'God is a Spirit and those who worship Him must worship Him in spirit and in truth'.

Throughout their history, as the Old Testament reveals, they had regularly been lured into false religions, falling into idolatry, and suffering greatly in consequence. Time and time again their leaders and prophets condemned their sinfulness and obstinacy, warning of dire consequences unless they returned to the one true God. It usually took some terrible disaster to make them acknowledge how completely they depended on God and his plans for them, before they turned away from paganism and showed remorse for their own ingratitude.

Following his encounter on Mount Sinai, Moses passed on to his fellow Jews the strict instructions he had been given by God in the Second Commandment, that they must keep themselves as a race apart in order to remain uncontaminated by the heathen communities amongst whom they lived.

> 'Thou shalt not make unto thee any graven image,
> or any likeness of any thing that is in heaven above
> or that is in the earth beneath, or that is in the water
> under the earth'.

Consequently, because in those times, the Jews were surrounded by graven images of all kinds, of so-called gods and goddesses, or one Caesar or another (not to mention images of various animals which were venerated by some pagan nations), any pictorial representation, be it painting, drawing or sculpture of the human form, was banned, as it could be construed as idolatry. And that is the reason why we know so little about the clothes worn by the Jewish people of those days, or how they looked: *there are no reliable records*.

However, on the subject of biblical clothing we should

take into consideration the many cultures which flourished in the region, Greeks, Romans, Persians and Assyrians among others, and which were bound to influence Jewish dress. The differences would have been in the jewellery and other decorative details, bearing in mind that according to rabbinical teaching, Jews were exhorted to dress modestly, avoiding luxuriousness on one hand, but on the other avoiding the appearance of beggarliness.

The main garment was a simple tunic, rather like an elongated T-shirt. It would have a rounded or V-shaped neckline, short or long sleeves, and could be full-length or just to the knee, though women always wore the former. In design and workmanship this tunic ranged from the very simple to the richly embroidered, sometimes with appliqué trimming, or studded with semi-precious stones, depending on the taste and wealth of the owner. The garment would be in woven wool for the cool seasons and woven linen for the warmer months, but curiously never a mixture of both, for this was forbidden under Jewish law.

The weaving would be carried out at home by the women of the family who had been trained since childhood, and the materials would be very colourful: blues, yellows, light greens, violet and other pastel shades for women; dark colours: greys, browns and green for men. The most sought-after was pure white, in spite of the constant laundering this demanded.

A wide band of material would often be tied around the waist of the tunic (especially in the case of men), and for further covering a piece of cloth, rectangular in shape, would be draped around the shoulders, or around one shoulder, very much in the style of the Greek stole or Roman toga. In the case of women, the drape might be fastened on one or even both shoulders with brooches that looked very much like our safety-pins, and the drapery could also be drawn over the hair for head-covering. In colder months, the drape would be made of warm material and swathed around the body.

Jewish men would sometimes wear an 'aba', a roomy over-garment open down the front and with wide sleeves.

It would usually be striped – in fact, stripes of various colours and widths were a major characteristic of Jewish design, and Joseph's coat of many colours is believed to have been just such a garment though of exceptionally beautiful and colourful design. There is a reminder of this today in the white prayer shawl known as a 'tallith', worn by Jewish men in the synagogues, which is edged with stripes in varying widths, generally blue, but sometimes black.

So important was drapery to the finished appearance of a person, that, just as wealthy, fashionable people in our era go to expensive tailors or couturiers, in those earlier times, men and women who could afford it would have their favourite drapers famous for their expertise in draping their clients' finest linen, wool or occasionally silk, in ever more intricate and elegant ways. For those with limited means, such as Mary and her family, it would have been very much a matter of do-it-yourself drapery.

Everyday footwear would have been sandals, similar to the simple leather-thonged ones still popular today, seen so often in summer. In the dusty conditions of the Middle East, feet would get very dirty over the course of a day; that is why they were washed so frequently, which was especially important for a people who have always given high priority to general hygiene (the Talmud goes into precise and demanding detail about personal and domestic cleanliness) so when we read about Jesus washing the feet of his apostles, we should see it against the background of what was a daily domestic custom.

What language did the Holy Family speak?

Aramaic was in general use because it was the common language throughout the Middle East, and it is the language that would have been used daily by Jesus, Mary, Joseph and the apostles, though Hebrew was the language of religion, government and the upper classes. Some parts of the Old Testament – the books of Daniel and Ezra – were written in Aramaic, as were the Babylonian and Jerusalem Talmuds, those lengthy books detailing every aspect of Jewish law and teaching which Our Lord would have known by heart. Greek too was widely spoken by Jewish people, especially those living in the Diaspora who would have known the Scriptures in Greek translation. It was also used in business and legal matter. Among all other foreign influences Greek culture was the most dominant.

The Betrothal
At the time of her betrothal to Joseph, Mary would have been in her teens (Jewish girls were considered to be of marriageable age when they were thirteen). A betrothal was similar to but more serious than modern-day engagements; it formed the first of the two parts of a Jewish marriage, and involved a formal undertaking in front of two witnesses, when the man would have to give his bride-to-be a simple ring or some other object that had to be of greater value than the smallest coin of the time – a *'perutah'*. While doing this, he would recite the traditional marriage formula in Hebrew or Aramaic: 'Behold, you are consecrated unto me with this and according to the law of Moses and Israel'.

This was followed by two blessings, one of which strongly emphasized that the betrothed pair were forbidden to live together until after the marriage proper of the second ceremony a year later. The significance of this for Mary and Joseph is as relevant to our understanding today as it was to the inner circle of the Holy Family more than two thousand years ago. I have come across a few Christian writers who, feeling impelled to spring to the defence of Mary's reputation, have stated it is insulting to claim she was unmarried when she became pregnant. Obviously they have never read the extract from St Luke's Gospel quoted at the beginning of this chapter, which leaves no room whatsoever for misunderstanding.

We do not know exactly when the Angel Gabriel contacted Joseph and then Mary with his awesome message but, under the circumstances, common sense has to be the guide in assuming that it would have been in the later stages of the year-long betrothal, shortly before the formal wedding ceremony when there would be no sign of Mary's condition. This was perfect timing by the Holy Spirit, and was essential not just for Mary and Joseph but also for her cousins, Elizabeth and Zechariah, who knew that the birth of their own son – itself something of a miracle in the natural order – was in some way going to be intimately connected with the virgin birth of their cousin Mary's baby who was destined to be the Messiah. This careful divine plan was essential, because if Our Lady had become pregnant *after* she had married Joseph, the profound meaning of the virgin birth would have been lost to all future generations.

It tells us something about his innate goodness that Joseph's first instinct, when he learnt about Mary's pregnancy, was to protect her, for as noted in Matthew 1:19, 'And her husband Joseph, being a just man, and unwilling to put her to shame, resolved to send her away quietly'. But he was stopped from pursuing this line of thought by an angel who appeared to him in a dream, and told him not to be afraid to take Mary as his wife, as it was by the power of the Holy Spirit that she had conceived the child.

This great shared secret must have strengthened the bond between Joseph and Mary; yet however privileged and overjoyed they felt, they would also have been under enormous strain, especially as both were well aware that for an unmarried girl to become pregnant was to bring immediate shame not only on her but on her entire family.

Marriage
The second ceremony, the full marriage service with all its traditional solemnity, went ahead, and by this time perhaps Elizabeth and Zechariah would have been let into Mary and Joseph's secret, as there seems to have been a fairly short interval between the wedding and Mary's visit to Elizabeth.

In ancient times, when the Jews were a nomadic people living in tents, before King David had decided on Jerusalem as their capital and they began to live in settled communities, their weddings would take place in a tent which was called a *'huppah'*. The bride in her beautiful wedding garments would be led to this bridal tent with great ceremony, singing and dancing, flowers strewn in her path. Over the centuries, as people began to live in houses, the custom was modified, and a room in the bridegroom's house would be specially decorated for the occasion, but it would still be referred to as a *huppah*. Even today, the word is still used for a Jewish marriage ceremony in a synagogue, which takes place under an ornate canopy symbolizing an ancient tent of Israel.

In Our Lady's time, as in ours, the marriage ceremony would be followed by a lively wedding party, feasting and dancing, which could go on for days. A curious detail: unlike our custom where the bride's parents organize the wedding festivities, in those ancient times it was the bridegroom who had to make all the arrangements, and he was expected to devote at least three days to the preparations, so Joseph must have been kept extremely busy. Perhaps it helped to take his mind off the extraordinary situation in which he found himself, as he was probably still in a state of shock at learning that not only was his betrothed expecting a baby, but that the infant was the long-awaited Messiah.

Meditation

This was a world of rich and powerful heathen kings and leaders plotting and fighting for more riches, more power, more self-glory. Meanwhile, in an unimportant region of Judea, a young woman had placed her trust in the God who created the universe: that same God who was about to enter our space-time continuum as a Jewish male, the Saviour of mankind, thanks to the trusting co-operation of his mother-to-be. *That* is where the real power in the world lay: with Mary in Nazareth.

Mary is God's most important created being whose assent to and co-operation with God's will was absolutely essential for the salvation of mankind, but she is not a goddess: divinity belongs to God alone. This may seem self-evident, but with great wisdom, and aware of the dangers of a blurring of perception that from time to time arises on this matter, the chapter on Our Lady in the Second Vatican Council's document, *Lumen Gentium*,

> strongly urges theologians and preachers of the word of God to be careful to refrain as much from all false exaggeration as from too summary an attitude in considering the special dignity of the Mother of God ... Let the faithful remember moreover that true devotion consists neither in sterile or transitory affection, nor in a certain vain credulity, but proceeds from true faith, by which we are led to recognise the excellence of the Mother of God, and we are moved to a filial love towards our mother and to the imitation of her virtues. (*LG* 67).

Second Joyful Mystery

The Visitation

... In those days Mary arose and went with haste into the hill country, to a city of Judah, and she entered the house of Zechariah and greeted Elizabeth. And when Elizabeth heard the greeting of Mary, the babe leaped in her womb; and Elizabeth was filled with the Holy Spirit and she exclaimed with a loud cry, 'Blessed are you among women, and blessed is the fruit of your womb! And why is this granted me, that the mother of my Lord should come to me? For behold, when the voice of your greeting came to my ears, the babe in my womb leaped for joy. And blessed is she who believed that there would be a fulfilment of what was spoken to her from the Lord.'
Luke 1:39–45

Significantly, Luke's Gospel begins not with the Visitation of Mary to her cousin Elizabeth, but with a much earlier visit – that of Gabriel to Zechariah, where Luke describes the dire consequence for the elderly priest when in bewilderment he questioned the angelic messenger's announcement that he was to become a father at his advanced age. 'I am Gabriel, who stand in the presence of God; and I was sent to speak to you, and to bring you this good news. And behold, you will be silent and unable to speak until the day that these things come to pass, because you did not believe my words, which will be fulfilled in their time' (Luke 1:19–20). It was to be six months before Mary learnt about her cousin's pregnancy, when Gabriel told her about it at the Annunciation.

These two incidents are significant because they stress the spiritual as well as the family connection in the destinies of Jesus and John. Sometimes, the crucial relevance of John the Baptist's role in our salvation is not fully appreciated; he seems in a way to be distanced from the apostles who were physically so close to Jesus throughout his public life. Yet from the moment of his conception John had been chosen by God to be the man who in time would become known as the last prophet of the Old Testament, as well as the precursor of Christ the Messiah.

As we know, soon after Mary heard the astonishing news about Elizabeth she swiftly made arrangements to go and stay with her during the final months of the latter's pregnancy. This must have happened very soon after the formal marriage of Joseph and Mary: if it had been later, her own pregnancy would be in a more advanced state by the time she returned to Nazareth, and this would have caused gossip among those who realized that her condition pre-dated the marriage.

Now here we have to be realistic about the dates and times of a number of events in the Gospels. In our age of hi-tech communications systems, it is thought-provoking to recall the difficulties of the apostles who had to record as much as they could about the hectic three years of Christ's public ministry by painstakingly writing everything by hand, so that these accounts would eventually form the base for spreading the Kingdom of God: the New Testament. The Jewish measuring of time was complex and differed somewhat from that used by the Romans; understandably, this has resulted in occasional uncertainties in dating and timing some parts of the Gospels, and although it was known in Israel that hours could be divided into minutes and seconds, it is considered unlikely that the actual method for doing so had yet reached this region. Therefore, appointments with people, times of arrivals and departures had to be flexible; indeed the exact time – as we understand the term – of *any* event was difficult to pin down. But if we assume that the birth of Jesus occurred in December–January, we can calculate that the Visitation took place some time in April.

So how exactly did Our Lady make the tiring journey from Nazareth to the place traditionally associated with the birth of John the Baptist, Ein Karem, nearly 100 miles away? Certainly not by camel, although this was the main means of transport in the constant comings and goings on the busy national and international caravan routes. Mary's journey, over Judea's rugged terrain, would have taken between a week to ten days and the best method by far (perhaps the *only* method) would have been by donkey.

The use of donkeys among Jewish people in the time of the Holy Family went back to their more ancient era when they left Egypt and settled in Canaan, the land promised to them by God, a pagan country which became Israel (and, incidentally, included most of what is now known as Jordan, as well as the southern tips of Syria and Lebanon). Naturally, the first requirement was to build homes for themselves, and soon mud-brick villages sprouted over the countryside. Then, following the example of their Canaanite neighbours, they acquired their own domestic animals, especially donkeys, to help in the daily round.

This humble beast of burden (used even today in some parts of the Middle East) had the two most important characteristics for hilly country: stamina and sure-footedness, both indispensable in negotiating the twists, turns and uneven surfaces of the paths into the hills. Families became as attached to their donkeys as people are today to their cats and dogs; they would give them names and often decorate them with coloured beads and wool, and even share living quarters – the creatures having their own section on the ground floor, part of which had been raised into a combined living and sleeping area for the family.

Not only were donkeys the most valuable and versatile members of a family's collection of domestic animals, they were also the cheapest to feed. In their colonies, the

Romans even imposed taxes on donkeys, and it is believed that this applied in Judea, the level of payments depending on whether they were for business or private use. In fact, the sturdy, hard-working creatures had many uses, from being carriers of provisions and other freight, to providing secure transport for young children who were hauled along in sacks slung on each side of the animal. And it was not only the poorer families who depended to such an extent on the sturdy little donkeys; it was also a popular way of travel for highborn ladies, and they, like the highest born lady of all, Mary, followed the four thousand-year-old custom of sitting sideways on the animal.

Generally this mode of transport was so comfortable that women would often do a bit of spinning on the journey to while away the time, rather as women today might take advantage of a long car or train journey to do some knitting.

Mary would not have travelled alone; very few people did in those times unless the journey was a short one, for travelling presented a variety of hazards, including storms, oppressive heat, and the ever-present danger of robbers and bandits. So whether Joseph was able to accompany her or not, Mary would most definitely have been with other travellers, some of whom may already have been familiar with the tricky route through the Judean hills to Ein Karem.

When she set out on her journey in April, the countryside would have been fresh and green with the advent of spring, the scent of wild flowers and herbs beginning to perfume the air of the hill country as the group rode on and looked for suitable spots where they could stop to rest and eat, relaxing for a while before going on their way. When at last Mary arrived at her cousin's home, she would obviously have been tired after the long, slow journey but suffused with excitement on thinking of all she and Elizabeth had to tell each other; certainly Elizabeth had already been told about Mary's miraculous pregnancy, as is evident in her loving greeting to her young cousin. But it is in Our Lady's response that we encounter her profound familiarity with the Old Testament, which, like the majority of religious Jewish people at the time, she most likely knew by heart; indeed, her beautiful Magnificat virtually paraphrases many parts of Jewish scripture.

> My soul magnifies the Lord,
> and my spirit rejoices in God my Saviour,
> for he has regarded the low estate of his handmaiden.
> For behold, henceforth all generations will call me
>   blessed;
> for he who is mighty has done great things for me,
> and holy is his name.   (Luke 1:46–9)

It is clear from the final section of her prayer that Mary understood her destiny was to bear the Jewish Messiah.

> He has helped his servant Israel,
> in remembrance of his mercy,
> as he spoke to our fathers,
> to Abraham and to his posterity for ever.

After their initial greetings, when Elizabeth made it clear that she knew about Mary's pregnancy, she would surely have explained to her young cousin why she had not let her know about her own pregnancy. We know that for five months Elizabeth 'retired' and this deliberate decision to withdraw from the community may have been for a number of reasons; first, worry that her condition would cause tittle-tattle among the neighbours – an elderly woman, known to be barren, suddenly expecting a baby: second, that at her age, something might go wrong in the early stages of pregnancy; and third, the embarrassment about her husband's muteness. Nine months of silence from Zechariah must have been a strain for Elizabeth, and difficult to explain to the local Jewish community ('An angel did it?!'), especially as he would have been unable to perform his schedule of priestly duties at the Temple in Jerusalem.

The naming of the baby boy took place (as it still does in

Jewish families) at the same time as the circumcision, that is, eight days after the birth, and it would have been a very festive occasion attended by family and friends at Zechariah's rather grand house, which was the norm for priests of the Temple. Opinion is divided on whether Mary stayed on for the celebrations or whether she returned to Nazareth before they took place, but it would be at odds with the strong bonds of Jewish family life that Mary, who had looked after Elizabeth for three months, should leave before the circumcision and naming party. It is rather more likely that Joseph came up from Nazareth for the event and then took Mary back with him, particularly as at that stage Mary was in her third month of pregnancy, and the return journey would have been particularly arduous under the hot June sun.

When we wonder why Gabriel was so insistent that Elizabeth's son should be called John, it is interesting to note that in Hebrew the name means 'Yahweh is gracious'. But the neighbours, not knowing this, and singularly unimpressed with the choice of a name which had no family connections, were so irritated by Elizabeth's insistence that they appealed to the father for support. What followed startled them, for not only did Zechariah confirm, in writing, that his son's name *was* to be John, but the moment he did so, his speech suddenly returned. The news ran like wildfire throughout the hill country of Judea, and the community recognized that the Lord was with Zechariah, while amongst themselves they asked 'What then will this child be?'

About John's boyhood we know even less than we do about that of Jesus, but as Zechariah was known to be deeply devout, John would have been brought up with a thorough grounding in the Bible and the Torah, and the sacramental aspects of Judaism, especially as his father may have expected that his beloved son would eventually become a priest, since the priesthood was hereditary. On the other hand, Zechariah may have remembered the exact words from Gabriel about John's future:

'And he will turn many of the sons of Israel to the
    Lord their God,
and he will go before him in the spirit and power of Elijah,
to turn the hearts of the fathers to the children,
and the disobedient to the wisdom of the just,
to make ready for the Lord a people prepared.'

(Luke 1:16–17)

We do not know if the two children ever met at family or religious gatherings, but in sixteenth-century art, John is often represented as Christ's playmate, and this was a popular motif in some of Raphael's Madonna portraits.

Meditation

It is not difficult to imagine the thoughts uppermost in Mary's mind as she made the long journey to Ein Karem: excitement, obviously, about her own condition, but also elation to discover that God's plan involved a member of her own family, Elizabeth, barren, yet soon to be blessed with a son in her old age. She may have wondered what was the connection, and how the two boys were destined to work together to carry out God's will. Later in her life, when Mary fully realized that her son was the promised Messiah, she may have recalled her thoughts in those early months of her own pregnancy, and marvelled at the way that God from the beginning of time had planned to link the cousins in his plan for the salvation of all mankind.

Third Joyful Mystery

The Nativity

In those days a decree went out from Caesar Augustus that all the world should be enrolled. This was the first enrolment when Quirinius was governor of Syria. And all went to be enrolled, each to his own city. And Joseph also went up from Galilee, from the city of Nazareth, to Judea, to the city of David, which is called Bethlehem, because he was of the house and lineage of David, to be enrolled with Mary, his betrothed, who was with child. And while they were there the time came for her to be delivered. And she gave birth to her first-born son and wrapped him in swaddling cloths, and laid him in a manger, because there was no place for them in the inn.

Luke 2:1–7, 17–18

Since original sin was the consequence of the Fall, for which God, admonishing Eve, told her: 'I will greatly multiply your pain in childbearing; in pain you shall bring forth children', it would be illogical and unreasonable to believe that Mary, the only created being to be born without original sin, should have suffered pain during childbirth. It is more probable that the event was one of great joy for her. An interesting point is that various mystics have said that this is exactly what they 'saw' in their visions.

We know that Joseph had to return to his birthplace because of the census; we know too, that he was of King David's lineage, but what is gradually being revealed through modern biblical scholarship is that Mary herself may also have been in the Davidic line too; some writers even point out that because there were such close bonds between those from the same tribe, it is very likely that Joseph may have been a kinsman of Our Lady.

The fact that Jesus was born in a stable because there was no room for him at the inn, should be put into context: it was probably better that it should have been so. The inns of those days were not cosy lodgings; they were usually places where the transport animals were kept at ground level in an open square, while 'rooms', which in some cases were more like cubicles, and generally unfurnished, lined a surrounding gallery. On the occasion of the census they would have been packed with people from all over the region who had crowded into the small village. Noise, dirty conditions, lack of privacy – the worst kind of environment for any young girl giving birth, but especially for the mother of Our Saviour. The stable, it is now agreed, was a cave where domestic animals were kept; away from all the crowds, it would have been quieter, cleaner and cosier. The stone manger was carved out of the wall and close to the ground, and would have been carefully lined with fresh straw, and Mary and Joseph would have brought with them the necessary articles for the birth. There would have been other Jewish women there, at the inn, or in the district, who undoubtedly would have attended Mary at the birth.

Immediately after birth, Jewish babies were always wrapped in swaddling clothes. Indeed Ezekiel, in the Old Testament, stated it was a curse to be deprived of them. But before the swaddling, the baby would have been rubbed all over with salt, then Mary would have placed him on a square piece of cloth, his head in one corner and his feet in the opposite corner. The cloth would be folded over his sides and feet, and then, using plain strips of cloth (wealthy people sometimes used embroidered strips) she would have tied his tiny hands to his sides. A cloth strip would also be carefully drawn under the infant's chin – and for a very sound reason; it taught the baby to breathe through its nose. He would then be placed in the manger. During the day, the swaddling was loosened, and the child rubbed with olive oil and dusted with powdered myrtle leaves, in the same way that modern mothers use talcum powder.

We are told that soon after the birth, the shepherds made their appearance: they were awake in the fields, keeping nightwatches over their flocks. But these few lines do not reveal the intricacy of God's plan to ensure that the Nativity should become known far and wide in the Jewish community and beyond.

Like most people, I have always pictured the shepherds wandering over the fields looking after their flocks, but it seems it wasn't quite like that, and it is from information in the Mishnah, part of Jewish Talmudic writing, that a clearer picture emerges. Not far from Bethlehem, on the road leading to Jerusalem, there was a tower called Migdal Eder – the name means 'the watchtower of the flock' – and it was from there, not at ground level as generations have believed, but from a good vantage point, that the shepherds would have watched their sheep, thousands of them, who were destined for sacrifice at the temple.

It was at the watchtower, too, that they would have been found by the angel who brought them the good news: 'this will be a sign for you: you will find a babe wrapped in swaddling cloths and lying in a manger' – a message immediately followed by the appearance of a multitude of the heavenly army 'praising God and saying, "Glory to God in the highest, and on earth peace among men with whom he is pleased!"' (Luke 2:13–14).

And then we come to the next stage in the divine plan for the shepherds; humble they may have been in the sight of men, but they were to provide a key element in the spreading of the good news. First, the shepherds lost no time in going to Bethlehem to visit the infant Jesus. On seeing him, they discovered the truth of what had been told them about the child, 'and all who heard it wondered at what the shepherds told them'. It is this last line that is so significant, because 'all who heard it' were the huge crowds of devout Jewish men and women who would be in Jerusalem to offer sacrifice for their sins or for special intentions at the temple, and would therefore be in close daily contact with the shepherds. When they had finished their business in Jerusalem, the shepherds returned home, giving praise and glory to God, so they were also able to spread the news in other parts of the country.

Meditation

In spite of all our modern high-powered information technology, communications professionals know that the best system of all is by word of mouth; hearing the news from someone who has seen, used, experienced something at first hand. And over two thousand years ago three shepherds were chosen by God to do just that, to inform the Jewish people about the birth of their Messiah. And it was probably on this occasion that the prophetess Anna, who lived day and night in the temple, first heard about the Nativity, though it would be over six weeks before she and Simeon would see the divine baby for themselves.

How joyful it must have been at that wonderful time –

and how the news must have spread like wildfire throughout the region before it was overtaken by the events to come during the early childhood of Jesus.

Fourth Joyful Mystery

The Presentation

And at the end of eight days, when he was circumcised, he was called Jesus, the name given by the angel before he was conceived in the womb. And when the time came for their purification according to the law of Moses, they brought him up to Jerusalem to present him to the Lord (as it is written in the law of the Lord, 'Every male that opens the womb shall be called holy to the Lord') and to offer a sacrifice according to what is said in the law of the lord, 'A pair of turtledoves or two young pigeons.'

Luke 2:21–5

The Presentation of Our Lord coincided with the end of the forty-day purification of Mary as set down in the Jewish scriptures in the book Leviticus:

And the Lord said to Moses, 'Say to the people of Israel, If a woman conceives, and bears a male child, then she shall be unclean seven days: as at the time of her menstruation, she shall be unclean. And on the eighth day the flesh of his foreskin shall be circumcised. Then she shall continue for thirty-three days in the blood of her purifying; she shall not touch any hallowed thing, nor come into the sanctuary, until the days of her purifying are completed.'

(Lev. 12:1–4)

During the forty days, Mary would have remained at home in Bethlehem, where presumably, by then, the Holy Family were more suitably lodged. Then, at the appointed time, they would have made the comparatively short journey to the temple in Jerusalem where they presented the infant to God to conform with the law that the first-born male child is sacred to the Lord, then, following custom, but being of modest means, they offered up the sacrifice of either two turtle doves or two pigeons. But it was a presentation like no other, for in reality this was the Second Person of the Blessed Trinity entering his own home, and fulfilling the prophecies of the Annunciation, when Mary was told that her son would be known as the Son of the Most High, that the Lord God would give him the throne over the house of Jacob eternally, and that his kingdom would never have an end.

The elderly devout and learned Jew, Simeon, who had waited so long for the coming of the Messiah, came to the temple that day because the Holy Spirit had revealed to him that he would not die until he had seen the Christ, the Lord's anointed. That moment had arrived and, finding the Holy Family, he picked up the Messiah in his arms and blessed God, saying,

> 'Lord, now lettest thou thy servant depart in peace,
> according to thy word;
> for mine eyes have seen they salvation
> which thou hast prepared in the presence of all peoples,
> a light for revelation to the Gentiles,
> and for glory to thy people Israel.'

Mary and Joseph 'marvelled' at these words, but after Simeon had blessed them both, he had a sombre message for Mary, foretelling her future sorrows:

> 'Behold, this child is set for the fall and rising of many in
>   Israel,
> and for a sign that is spoken against
> (and a sword will pierce through your own soul also),
> that thoughts out of many hearts may be revealed.'

Finally, they were approached by the prophetess, Anna, a very elderly woman who stayed at the temple night and day, fasting and praying to God. Looking at last on the Messiah she had been praying for, she gave thanks to God, and later spoke of the child to all those who had been waiting for the deliverance of Israel.

Meditation

Following the momentous event of the Presentation, the
Holy Family returned to Bethlehem. It is easy to imagine the
impression left in the hearts and minds of Mary and Joseph
by the events that occurred in Jerusalem, and although both
of them knew beyond doubt that Jesus was the Messiah, the
implications must have been too immense to grasp initially.
And Mary, like any loving mother, was bound to have felt a
tremor of misgiving at Simeon's prophecy, making her
become even more protective of her baby; perhaps both
Mary and Joseph were puzzled about Simeon's reference to
the Gentiles and wondered what relevance it could have to
the Jewish Messiah.

After the Presentation, the Holy Family returned to Bethlehem, during which time they were visited by three digni-
taries from the East who came bearing gifts. Matthew tells
us that when King Herod heard about this, it troubled not
only him but 'all Jerusalem' as well. So much, in fact, that he
assembled all the chief priests and scribes and asked them
where the Christ would be born. They told him that according to prophecy it was to be in Bethlehem. Herod arranged
a secret meeting with the three visitors from East, the 'wise
men', and, appearing to be supportive, he asked them to let
him know when they found the child so that he, too, could
go and worship him. This was a statement which they took
in good faith, but after their visit to Mary and Jesus, they
were warned in a dream not to contact Herod, so they
returned home by a different route.

Herod's fury, as we know, resulted in his order for the
terrible slaughter of the innocents when every male child
in Bethlehem under two years old was to be killed. But
before this began, Joseph was warned by an angel in a
dream to take Mary and the child immediately to Egypt,
'... and remain there till I tell you; for Herod is about to
search for the child, to destroy him'. Thus began some
years of wandering in Egypt, a country that had a flour-
ishing Jewish population, where the Holy Family would
be accepted into the community, and Joseph, as a skilled
carpenter, could find steady employment.

Although the Scriptures do not – and could not at the time – trace the travels of the Holy Family in Egypt, the Coptic Church has documented and mapped the places visited by Joseph, Mary and their child, a tortuous journey from Assiut in the south to the Mediterranean coast in the north, together with the sites of numerous Coptic Churches marking these places. Most of the churches are named after the Holy Family or Mary the Virgin.

A few years later, when Herod died, the angel, as promised, appeared again to Joseph in a dream and told him that it was now safe to return to Israel (according to the Coptic documents they did so via the southern route); but when he learnt that Judea was now being ruled by Archelaus who was as bloodthirsty as his predecessor, Joseph decided to take Mary and Jesus back to Our Lady's region: Nazareth in Galilee, which now came under a different ruler. And there at last the Holy Family was able to settle down to a normal Jewish family life, a move that incidentally fulfilled the ancient prophecy about the Messiah, that 'He shall be called a Nazarene'.

So young herself, Mary found that during those precious early years of her son, when she might have expected to nurture him in the safety of her own home, she and Joseph had to escape with the infant Jesus before he became a victim of Herod's murder of the innocents. Far from family and friends, the Holy Family would have been a self-contained unit, living their secret life in a foreign country, although there were many Jewish communities in Egypt who undoubtedly would have welcomed the newcomers and helped them to find somewhere to live, and work for Joseph.

Mary's contemplative nature would have absorbed every experience of these turbulent, insecure years, and she would have been in perfect union with God, trusting and utterly dependent on him as always, knowing that she and Joseph had been given the most important responsibility of any other two people in the history of the world: to love and protect the Messiah.

Fifth Joyful Mystery

The Finding of Jesus in the Temple

*Now his parents went to Jerusalem every year at the feast of the
Passover. And when he was twelve years old, they went up according
to custom; and when the feast was ended, as they were returning, the
boy Jesus stayed behind in Jerusalem. His parents did not know it, but
supposing him to be in the company they went a day's journey, and
they sought him among their kinsfolk and acquaintances; and when
they did not find him, they returned to Jerusalem, seeking him. After
three days they found him in the temple, sitting among the teachers,
listening to them and asking them questions; and all who heard him
were amazed at his understanding and his answers.*

Luke 2:41–7

For weeks before setting off for Jerusalem for the Passover,
Mary, like all Jewish women, would have been preparing
for the long caravan journey to Jerusalem: provisions for
the four or so days of travel, clothing, provender for the
donkeys and any other animals involved in the transport,
as well as the basic essentials for life on the road. Jesus was
twelve years old on this occasion, and it is believed this
would have been his first visit to the temple since his
Presentation. In fact, people who lived at a long distance
from Jerusalem, that is more than 30 kms away, were
exempt from the obligation of making the journey, as were
women, though Mary had always accompanied Joseph.

During the days of travel there would have been stops
for food, rest and refreshment, and there would have been
intermingling between families and friends, especially
those who might not have seen each other for some time,
as they caught up on each other's news: the usual gossip
about births, marriages and deaths since last they met.

As Nazareth was at the crossroads of caravan routes,
Mary, Joseph and Jesus would have been accustomed to the
constant comings and goings of camels, asses and horses
with their burdens and their owners who were following
the busy trade routes from various parts of the Middle East.
But the crowded roads and paths to Jerusalem at Passover

would have been an astonishing sight. At the time, there were between five and seven million Jewish people in the Roman Empire alone, as well as numerous others who lived beyond Rome's eastern borders, and huge numbers of them went to Jerusalem for this most important feast of the year. The historian, Josephus, claimed that millions of people crowded into the city, and though this is believed to be something of an exaggeration, there were certainly many hundreds of thousands.

It has been said that the roads in New Testament times were much the same as those in nineteenth-century Europe: people depended on riding animals or using vehicles that were pulled along by animals, the main difference being that roads at the time of the Holy Family were in a far better condition than those eighteen centuries later. That, of course, was due to the skilled Roman road builders. Some Passover pilgrims walked to Jerusalem, while those from other parts of the Mediterranean would come by sea. As the journey progressed on its way there would be an increasingly lively atmosphere, singing, story-telling and increasing joy as they approached Jerusalem to celebrate one of the greatest and most miraculous events in their ancient history: God's intervention in ensuring their freedom from Egyptian slavery.

Then suddenly, there it was – the glorious view they had been longing to see – shining like a huge white marble and gold jewel high on its hill, the Temple of Jerusalem: a building of huge dimensions with its seemingly endless series of porticoes and colonnades, courtyards and columns. The Court of Israel, for instance, was some 150 ft high above steps that had to be climbed laboriously. One bronze gate alone needed twenty men to open it, and some porticoes were 50 ft wide with colonnades so large that halls and rooms had been built in them.

The temple was staffed by about 18,000 men, ranging from the high priests and ordinary priests – who came from all over Israel to carry out their rota of a week's service – to the Levites, the lowest order who undertook more menial duties. Over Passover, they would all have had their work cut out to cope with the flood of pilgrims who crowded into the inns and hostels attached to the temple, visitors from different countries who spoke different languages but were united by their faith.

Families would join together to buy a lamb or kid for sacrifice if they had not brought the animal with them. The slaughter would be carried out in the temple courtyard, and the priests would gather the blood in cups and pour it at the foot of the altar. Throughout these hours, there would have been great excitement and noise, against a background of trumpets and the occasional outburst of sung prayers. The sacrificed animal would then be taken to the house where the Paschal meal was to be held, and it would be roasted, skewered on a rod of pomegranate wood.

At sunset, the family would sit around the table and the Paschal meal would begin, interspersed at precise intervals by a series of prayers, meditations, psalms and the account of how Moses, the Jewish foundling brought up by an Egyptian princess, led his people out of slavery; of God's miraculous parting of the Red Sea; the plagues visited on Egypt when the Pharaoh obstinately refused to let the Jewish people leave his country, and their ultimate joy when their return was eventually accomplished. Above all, the Paschal meal is directed at the younger members of the family, for it was (and still is) the way of teaching Judaism's early history to the new generation so that it may never be forgotten. A touching highlight of Passover, which goes back to the time of Moses, occurs when one of the young children stands up and asks what is the meaning of this service; to this the father, in simple language, relates the entire history of Israel from Abraham down to the deliverance from Egypt, and the giving of the Law. It is moving to think that on that particular Passover, the boy Jesus may have been the youngster asking these familiar questions of Joseph, the wonderful man who was entrusted by God with the awesome responsibility of bringing up the boy as his son. No matter what the circumstances of Jewish families might be, education has always been regarded as of major importance, and in biblical times there was compulsory education for all children above the age of six. This was considered to be so important that the Talmud states it was unlawful to live in a place where there was no school. During his earliest years, Jesus would have been taught by Joseph, for a child was expected to have read the bible by the age of five, learnt the Mishnah at ten, at thirteen years to follow the commandments, and at fifteen years to be studying the Talmud.

After the Paschal meal, the Holy Family stayed on in Jerusalem for the full eight days of the Passover period, and when they started back on their return journey to Nazareth, they would probably have been both elated and tired after all the emotional excitement of the past days. It was quite normal that during the day youngsters could go and spend time with relatives or play with friends in the caravan trail, but they knew they had to return to their families at night. The shock and fear that Mary and Joseph experienced when their son did not come back on that first night out is beyond imagination. Terrible thoughts of what might have happened to him would have passed through their minds, as they returned to Jerusalem to look for Jesus, retracing all the places where they hoped to find him.

Bearing in mind the sheer immensity of the temple, it must have been a gruelling undertaking; having to climb the steep steps up to each part of the temple where Jesus might be found; walking the exhausting length and breadth of the huge areas between the porticoes and colonnades; negotiating their way through the crowds who had stayed on for a few days, and searching among the groups sitting around learned rabbis discussing, through the accepted method of question and answer, everything to do with the tenets and traditions of the Jewish faith. Finally, on the third day of their desperate search, they came across a group of doctors of the law, who on Saturdays and high holidays met with their disciples to teach them the significance of the sacred

Scriptures. And there in the midst of these learned adults, the boy Jesus was calmly astonishing them all, especially Mary and Joseph, not just by his knowledge, but by his authority.

Our Lady's first words were spontaneous, utterly human and understandable, expressing a combination of indescribable relief and incomprehension that Jesus should apparently have been careless about their fears for him: 'Son, why have you treated us so? Behold, your father and I have been looking for you anxiously.' The response must have shaken both Mary and Joseph. 'How is it that you sought me? Did you not know that I must be in my Father's house?' (Luke 2:48–9). But neither Mary nor Joseph understood these words – not then.

Meditation

Occasionally people feel uneasy, almost guilty, in thinking that Jesus was being rather cheeky to his parents. Certainly it was not what they expected: not a word of apology for worrying them so much (though we can rest assured that what Mary's son said was delivered tenderly, lovingly and with a smile) but this incident has profound spiritual significance. There was a certain play on words in Jesus's reply. When Mary mentioned his father, Joseph, her son swiftly pointed out that he needed to be in the place which belongs to his Father. Suddenly, both Mary and Joseph were faced with the reality of what they had both been told by Gabriel, and later by Simeon and Anna. But over the years since the birth of Jesus, those extraordinary events may have somehow been submerged in their busy daily domestic lives. Perhaps the only way they had been able to live as conventional Jewish parents was to put the miracle at the back of their minds. After all, he was only a child; there would be plenty of time to think of his future once he became an adult. All they could do was to love and bring up this child with a special destiny: to be the promised Messiah. But what this actually would mean, neither could know, though the traditional belief was that the advent of the Messiah would introduce a golden age for their nation and the rescuing of their land from foreign rule.

From that moment when Jesus was found in the temple, Mary's 'pondering' entered a new phase which deepened throughout the rest of her life as she gradually came to understand the miraculous reality of her situation and the responsibility given to her by God. And from then on, 'his mother kept all these things in her heart'.

Mary and Joseph were jolted by the words of Jesus into the reminder of who he was, and in a way this entire episode has relevance to our own lives. It is so easy to take our faith, and the truths we know, for granted; to pray automatically, to meditate automatically, especially to pray the Rosary automatically, and perhaps sometimes we need to be stopped in our tracks and be reminded how salvation was made possible for us.

5

The Five Sorrowful Mysteries

When we come to consider the Sorrowful Mysteries of the Rosary, we enter a territory so dark, that in time (if we are properly focused on what we are praying and thinking) our perceptions of the evil voluntarily suffered by Our Lord will result in gratitude beyond words for all he did for us, and in a deepening of our own spiritual lives, as well as encouragement in our trials, as we travel towards the joy of promised salvation.

For the five decades of these searing Mysteries I have drawn upon three sources: first and foremost the Gospels, then the most up-to-date forensic evidence retrieved from the Holy Shroud, and finally, the private revelations of four mystics: St Bridget of Sweden who lived in the fourteenth century; the Spanish mystic, Venerable Maria d'Agreda of the seventeenth century; German mystic, Anne Catherine Emmerich of the nineteenth century, and Teresa Neumann who died in the twentieth century.

What is so striking about the respective accounts of Christ's Passion given by these women is that though they lived at different times and in different places their descriptions coincide, not just with each other but with aspects of the evidence found on the Shroud. However we must remember that though private visions are not part of essential dogma, nor even of church teaching, they can be aids to the imagination in the life of prayer.

There had been testimonies of a Sacred Shroud from earliest Christian times, but it was not until 1352 that it first appeared in documented history as belonging to a feudal knight in northern France, and it was not until 1578 that the Shroud found a permanent home in Turin Cathedral. Three more centuries were to pass before its full significance was discovered, the by-product, as it were, of a royal decree.

The year was 1898 when King Umberto I of Savoy, in celebration of the fourth centenary of Turin Cathedral and the wedding of Crown Prince Victor Emanuel, granted a public viewing of the Shroud and allowed a photograph of it to be taken by an Italian lawyer, Secondo Pia. In his memoirs, Pia describes his reactions when he first saw the image emerge on the Shroud: 'Shut away in my darkroom, and absorbed in my work, I felt a surge of very strong emotion when I saw the Holy Face appear for the first time on a plate, which such clarity that I was dumbfounded.' In fact, it was on the negative that the extent of the wounds inflicted on the body were revealed, not on the positive, though stains on the latter were later identified as blood. That the image presents a photographic negative should discredit once and for all the allegation that it had been painted on to the material by some unknown artist four or five centuries ago. There was clearly no identifiable image on the shroud previously, so it would never have come to light without the later invention of photography.

From that moment, the Shroud has undergone comprehensive examinations, and in 1969, Umberto II of Savoy and Cardinal Michele Pellegrino, then Archbishop of Turin, formed a commission of leading scientific experts using the most up-to-date methods of investigation. But the term 'up-to-date' is misleading, for the pace of scientific and technological advances enjoys major breakthroughs from one year to another. For instance, in 1988, the laboratories of Oxford, Tucson and Zurich, under the auspices of the British Museum, after carbon-dating the Shroud, declared that their findings indicated it had originated some time between the thirteenth and fourteenth centuries. Naturally, this caused great dismay, but Monsignor Giulio Ricci, a man who for fifty years had dedicated himself to discovering the truth about the Shroud and had kept in close contact with the most important research centres in the world, did not accept these findings. The reasons he gave now seem to have been justified, for, while not questioning the expertise of the laboratories who carried out the carbon tests, more recent results show that the conclusions announced earlier did not take into account damage done to the Shroud through pollution and damage by fires over the centuries. Sadly, Monsignor Ricci (who came to be known as the 'Apostle of the Shroud') died before he could have the satisfaction of knowing this, but his spirit lives on in the Giulio Ricci Diocesan Centre for Study of the Holy Shroud (Sindonology) in Rome.

Examinations of the Shroud have included the use of infra-red rays, ultra-violet rays and X-ray spectography. We now know that the Shroud covered a man who was over 1.80m tall, and this fits well with the finding that the flat stone on which the body would have been placed in the sepulchre was 2.5m long and 1m wide – measurements which would have perfectly fitted a man whose height was 1.80m. It is interesting to note that in the sixth century, Justinian sent envoys to Jerusalem to establish the physical stature of Jesus as he wished to erect a cross of silver and gold corresponding to a person of the same height. As further confirmation of this, in the cloisters of St John Lateran there is a shrine purported to be of the same height as Christ, exactly 1.80m.

Another eminent expert, the botanist Silvano Scannerini, likens the mystery of the Shroud to a detective story which began two thousand years ago. He says that investigations have to cover a range of disciplines from biology to physics, forensic medicine to archaeology, from biblical exegesis to textile analysis. 'The problem we have to solve,' he says, 'if we are to understand exactly what the Shroud is, lies in the sphere of forensic medicine.' As an example, he points out that the material of the Shroud was made of flax and bears traces of other vegetable matter such as pollen, oils and spices, extracted from ancient medicinal plants which could have been partly responsible for the forming of the image on the material. In fact, flax was used two thousand years ago for burial garments as well as for the ritual clothing of Jewish priests.

When a 5,000 year-old frozen body was discovered in a remote mountainous region a few years ago, it was pollen that enabled forensic scientists to date its age. Astonishingly, pollen on garments or cloth cannot be removed, even by washing or cleaning. It remains indefinitely, until the garment or cloth itself is destroyed.

Scannerini has also emphasized that the techniques now available for more detailed study of the Shroud have been borrowed from a science that has only been developed in the past decade: molecular biology. But even at this stage, we have a staggering new piece of information: it seems that the group of the blood taken from the stains on the Shroud belong to the AB grouping. DNA tests are already taking place.

During the Holy Father's visit to Turin in the year 2000, he said, 'The Shroud forces questions to be raised about the sacred linen and the historical life of Jesus.' He emphasized that since it is not a matter of faith, the Church has no competence to pronounce on these questions. 'This task,' he added, 'is for the scientists who are continuing their investigations into the Shroud so that satisfactory answers may be found to the many questions about the sheet which according to tradition wrapped the body of Jesus after he was taken down from the cross.' But perhaps the Pope's most significant comment was that 'The Shroud is a challenge to our intelligence.'

The full impact of this remark will be appreciated if you consider carefully the extraordinary coincidence that there exists an ancient shroud which shows evidence of severe beatings, resulting in bloodshed, of a man carrying a heavy weight on his shoulders; of terrible wounds on his body; of a crown of cruel thorns; of his crucifixion, with nail marks on his wrists and feet; and of herbs and spices having been used on the body before it was placed in the shroud. All this tallies with Christ's sufferings as depicted in the Gospels. The revelations of the Mystics are private revelations and not a matter of faith, though the published information from their writings contained in this chapter was given an *Imprimatur*, and their insights tally with New Testament accounts. At present, it has not been proved beyond all possible doubt that the body in the Shroud was that of Jesus, but by using our intelligence, how can we but conclude that, so far, the evidence is overwhelming?

First Sorrowful Mystery

The Agony at Gethsemane

Then Jesus went with them to a place called Gethsemane, and he said to his disciples, 'Sit here, while I go yonder and pray.' And taking with him Peter and the two sons of Zebedee, he began to be sorrowful and troubled. Then he said to them, 'My soul is very sorrowful, even to death; remain here and watch with me.' And going a little farther he fell on his face and prayed, 'My Father, if it be possible, let this cup pass from me; nevertheless, not as I will, but as thou wilt.'

Matt. 26:36–9

Out of all the places in the Holy Land, the Garden of Gethsemane on the slopes of the Mount of Olives is, for many pilgrims, the most moving, for it has managed to escape the hubbub of some of the other Christian sites and its tranquillity invites meditation. Here one can easily understand why Jesus and his disciples would often got there to find some peace and quiet away from the clamour of the crowd.

I remember asking a Franciscan if the olive tree that has such a prominent place in the little garden was supposed to be the original one where Our Lord used to sit. He said that as the tree was so old, it was impossible to say, but even if it wasn't the tree known to Jesus, the present one would have been planted where the original one had died. Some time later, I learnt that just before an olive tree does eventually die, a new young shoot will spring up in its place.

Jerusalem in April is usually cold, and when Jesus paid his last visit to Gethsemane, it would have felt even colder to him with the foreknowledge of what would shortly happen to him. Our Lord did not even have the comfort of companionship from Peter, James and John who fell asleep throughout his interior suffering, but as Luke explains, the three disciples were overwrought with sorrow. Perhaps, in their despair, they cried themselves to sleep.

One of the most poignant moments in the betrayal that followed surely occurred when Jesus gently said to the chief priests, temple officers and scribes who had come to find him, 'When I was with you day after day in the temple, you did not lay hands on me. But this is your hour, and the power of darkness.' (Luke 22:53).

These men, the most powerful within the Jewish religious community, alarmed by the threat to their authority that Jesus represented, had come like thieves in the night to steal Jesus away from the ordinary Jewish people who were thronging to Our Lord to listen to his message of salvation. These priests and scribes who preached about the coming of the Messiah could not accept that the reality might be very different from what they expected. This was no nationalistic leader simply dedicated to restoring the power and glory of a prosperous Israel; Our Lord's purpose was to restore the Jewish soul, the soul that had been nurtured and protected by God throughout centuries of persecution and aggression. These influential men, who had the power of life and death over the Jewish people, spread the lie that Jesus had come to destroy the Law, deliberately ignoring Christ's own words, 'Think not that I have come to abolish the Law and the prophets; I have come not to abolish them but to fulfil them' (Matt. 5:17). This falsehood was used by them as a key to their policy of disinformation, whose dire consequences continue to this day.

Meditation

The name Gethsemane means 'oil press', indicating that at one time this small private property in an enclosed garden would have been the site for the crushing of the olives which grew so abundantly in the region, and according to some sources it may have belonged to the father of Mark, but if not to him, then to other friends of Jesus.

In this place of peace and quietness which had become a meeting spot for the Master and his little band of twelve, Jesus waited for the first act of treachery which would mark the beginning of his Passion. He already knew every detail of the physical agony that awaited him, but on this night at Gethsemane, he plumbed the depths of mental anguish which are beyond the worst we can possibly imagine as he bore the pain of and for all mankind, past, present and to come. Every result of original sin – every injustice, every evil, every disaster, natural and unnatural, the wickedness of tyrants who arise in every generation and cause the deaths of millions of innocent people, all the selfishness, greed, and corruption that destroys individuals and whole communities – all this engulfed his soul, as he suffered for every man, woman and child, including those not yet born. Like the olives that used to be crushed in the olive press to provide the best and purest oil, the Sacred Heart of Jesus was being crushed under the weight of all humankind's sins, to provide the salvation of us all.

Our Lady, as we know, was not present at Gethsemane, but one or other of the disciples would have rushed to tell her what had happened and that her Son had been arrested and taken away. The shock must have been devastating.

Most of us have experienced the feeling of helplessness when a loved one undergoes the torment of pain, physical or mental, so it does not take a great leap of the imagination to understand how Mary must have felt, for her pain would have been doubled by the knowledge that not only was something terrible being committed against her Son, but also something terrible was being committed against the Jewish people by their own leaders. She knew that, now Christ had been arrested and taken before Caiaphas, the high priest, the momentum of his destiny was approaching a major crisis.

Mary, who was such a devoted Jewess, and whose knowledge of the Talmud, the Torah, and all the traditions of Judaism was so comprehensive, would have been particularly anguished that Jesus stood accused of trying to destroy the Law, when his whole purpose was to protect it, to purify it. She knew, and understood better than anyone, that the wonderful inner spirituality of the Jews, that God so loved, had been turned by their religious leaders into a distortion of true belief by the imposition of endless legalistic and trivial rules which governed every action and detail of their daily lives.

How must she have felt when she realized that nothing would be allowed to curtail or interfere with the murderous intentions of those who purported to be the priests of God. Later she may have been told by the disciples that just before Our Lord was taken away he had told the priests, chief scribes and those who had come to arrest him that their time had come and had brought the powers of darkness. And her heart must have been close to breaking as she contemplated the results of the wickedness that was about to be carried out against her Son and against her own Jewish people.

Second Sorrowful Mystery

Jesus is Scourged

Then Pilate took Jesus and scourged him.
John 19:1–2

In all four Gospels, scourging is only mentioned briefly by the Evangelists. The reason for this is probably because, at the time, everyone knew what it involved. But only when we, in our time, take a closer look at this form of torture can we reach a fuller understanding of the reality.

According to reliable sources, the Romans introduced scourging, which they had imported from customs in their

Eastern provinces. It was used not just as a punishment in itself, but also to extract confessions, and – most cruel – as a preliminary punishment before carrying out the death penalty. Cicero condemned it as an unfit punishment for free men, and indeed, it was mainly reserved for slaves and criminals.

The original form of corporal punishment used by the Jewish authorities was beating by sticks or rods, but later this was changed to scourging, using a leather three-thonged whip attached to a handle, but they took care not to go too far when dealing with less serious crimes so that death did not ensue, especially when scourging those who seemed less likely to survive. However, women were not excluded from this beating.

Although Roman scourges were basically the same, they had added an extra refinement of cruelty: pieces of iron, zinc or other sharp objects on each thong which flayed the skin at every blow.

The victim was stripped to the waist and tied to a column or stake for what was the most usual sentence – forty strokes, less one, of the whip. This was not an arbitrary figure but a convenient one, because three soldiers would have administered the torture, each applying thirteen strokes. And this is believed to be what Jesus would have suffered; his skin torn to shreds, his flesh bleeding. This reflects some of the accounts of the scourging as revealed by the mystics already mentioned. For instance, St Brigid's revelations include the information that the scourges used on Jesus were tipped with sharp points turned in on themselves so that each stroke dug into and pulled back the flesh, and the severity of the beating exposed Our Lord's ribs. The Holy Shroud shows that Jesus was scourged back and front; this is also mentioned in Teresa Neumann's account, who writes that the men who scourged Christ resembled those who took him prisoner at Gethsemane. In a poignant note, she adds that what Jesus found hardest to bear was being deprived of all his garments. Generally, the soldiers who carried out scourging were not Romans but soldiers from the provinces, usually Syria, and one of the mystics mentions a Syrian as being among the most vicious in the beating of Jesus.

Catherine Emmerich and the Venerable Maria d'Agreda agree in their accounts that Jesus was struck in the face, and this coincides with the Shroud's evidence of his broken nose and swollen face. Both these mystics make it clear that the torturers were intent on, and succeeded in, mangling Our Lord's body so that it looked like 'One continuous wound', to the extent that the relays of torturers (six relays in all, according to these women) could not find any spot for further whipping. Yet they continued to beat him on top of his open wounds. So much blood and so many bruises prevented Our Lord from being able to see properly, and he was spat at by those who came to jeer and mock him: a detail mentioned by Matthew and Mark in their Gospels.

Meditation

Although the Sanhedrin had all authority in local administration and in everything to do with Jewish issues, under the Romans it also enjoyed extensive legal authority, and operated rather like a high court. It was also political and voted in its own laws. Above all, it was in total control of everything to do with the Jewish religion, so within the Roman province, Judea enjoyed not total, but partial, autonomy, and understandably it was to everyone's advantage that the High Priest, who was seen by the Jewish people as the very embodiment of the Law, should have a good working relationship with, if not a liking for, the Roman governor of the region. It was also in the latter's interest to ensure that no troubles arose among the Jewish community that could cause problems for Rome and thus reflect badly on Pontius Pilate's competence. There is no doubt of his deep dismay and sense of foreboding when he was asked to order the execution of a man whom he saw as being totally innocent of any crime, and it was therefore a great relief for him to learn that, as Jesus was a Galilean, he came under the jurisdiction of King

Herod Antipas; Pilate swiftly passed the problem on to the king, who on failing to persuade Jesus to perform some sort of miracle to back up all the stories he had heard about him, treated him contemptuously and sent him back to Pilate. There is an interesting detail in Luke's account: 'And Herod and Pilate became friends with each other that very day, for before this they had been at enmity with each other.'

Pilate had been manipulated into a corner: refuse the demands of the Sanhedrin and risk a major problem with Caesar (a terrifying prospect, because the Roman emperor at the time was the murderous Tiberius) or accede to the killing of an innocent man. There was no contest.

Thus began the scourging, the first act in the greatest drama in the history of the world, the shock waves of which will continue to send ripples throughout time until time itself becomes meaningless in the context of personal salvation.

The execution of Jesus was the result of collusion between the Jewish religious leaders, the Roman governor and the reigning king. All were equally guilty. The majority of the Jewish people in Judea had neither influence nor power, nor even sufficient knowledge of the facts to make effective protest. Many of them had already accepted Christ, and many thousands would follow. It is known that relatives of Jesus were still living in Nazareth at least until AD 250; they were the leaders of the Judeo–Christian community there, who still used former synagogues to worship Christ, and presumably where for centuries Mass would have been celebrated. Pilate's career was to end in disgrace six years later when his incompetence resulted in a peaceful religious protest turning into a massacre, and he was banished to Gaul, where it is believed he committed suicide, either by his own choice or on orders from Rome.

While Mary's relatives and friends gathered around and tried to comfort her on learning about the death sentence and scourging of her son, she probably just wanted to retreat into herself, and ponder on the destiny that was now rapidly unfolding. Did she think about the strange symmetry of Herod Antipas wanting to meet Jesus just as Antipas's late father, another Herod, had tried to hunt Jesus down and have him killed when he was just an infant? Did she begin to understand only too clearly what Simeon was referring to when he had spoken of a sword piercing her soul? And, for our part, can we place ourselves by her side in our prayers to offer her our love for those dark, bereft moments as the Passion began?

Third Sorrowful Mystery

The Crowning with Thorns

Then the soldiers of the governor took Jesus into the praetorium, and they gathered the whole battalion before him. And they stripped him and put a scarlet robe upon him, and plaiting a crown of thorns they put it on his head and put a reed in his right hand. And kneeling before him they mocked him, saying 'Hail, King of the Jews!'

Matt. 27:27–9

Some years ago, in southern Spain, when I was walking around some tropical gardens praying the Sorrowful Mysteries of the Rosary, I reached the Third Sorrowful Mystery, and tried to imagine what the thorns would have looked like; in my mind's eye I pictured them as being similar to those I had seen at home in the English countryside, but then I happened to glance down and there, right in front of me, was a thorn bush, its thorns between $2^1\!/\!2''$ and 3″ long (about $7^1\!/\!2$ cms); their vicious-looking spikes reminded me of thorns I had seen in South Africa. Subsequently I discovered that indeed this was a species found in tropical and semi-tropical countries, and also in Palestine. Known by its botanical name, *Sarcopoterium spinosum Schranz*, it has for scholars now replaced the *Paliurus spina-Christi*, a plant with a much smaller thorn, as the kind most likely to have been used for such a grim purpose.

At the Church of the Holy Cross in Rome, there are two thorns which have been taken from the external framework (kept as a relic at Notre Dame Cathedral in Paris) of what is believed to be the original crown. These thorns are over an inch long and very sharp, but experts have revealed that this is only part of the original thorn and the whole would have measured between two and three inches. Investigations on that part of the Shroud where the head would have been bound confirm that ordinary thorns could not have caused such deep wounds. Further forensic texts also revealed something totally unexpected: the crown of thorns was not the familiar circlet familiar for centuries in religious works of art: it was more a helmet or cap that had been pressed tightly down on the head of Jesus, resulting in 'innumerable' wounds all over his head, making blood run down his hair and on to his face and the back of his head.

Now here we come to an example of that mysterious conjunction where science and the invisible word seem to converge.

In 1926 Teresa Neumann wrote in her account of what she had observed in her visions: 'The crown of thorns which is now ready is placed on Our Lord's head like a helmet; it is not just a crown as we see it depicted in our pictures. One of the soldiers presses the crown of thorns firmly on His head. The blood flows down His whole face which shows signs of intense pain during this terrible treatment.'

Teresa died in 1962. It was not until more than twelve years after her death that information started to enter the public domain about investigations into the Shroud, and only in the late 1990s that the latest developments in forensic science produced the astonishing results of the botanic investigations mentioned in this chapter.

The Venerable Maria d'Agreda's description of her own visionary experience, mentions that the crown had 'big strong thorns with very sharp points and was pressed down with such force that many of the thorns pierced the skull'. She added that the pain from this was one of the greatest that the Son of God suffered in his Passion.

It has already been pointed out that there is no obligation for Catholics to accept private revelations, such as those mentioned in this book, even when their accounts were printed with an imprimatur and include one mystic who is a canonized saint; but here we are faced with this inexplicable arc of space and time that links a visionary observation of the Passion with the most up-to-date findings of scientific experts.

The reed that was thrust into Christ's hand by the soldiers was a tall cane-like plant, the kind used to make pens for writing on ancient papyrus scrolls. But first, the soldiers had stripped him and put a scarlet robe on him. John, in his Gospel, refers to the colour as purple, while Luke writes that before Herod sent Christ back to Pilate, he had arrayed him 'in gorgeous apparel'. And so Our Lord, in a state of utter degradation and such suffering that he was barely able to stand, was draped in the luxurious garb of a monarch and a mockery of a crown, and then brought to face the howling mob, as Pilate declaimed with cutting sarcasm: 'Here is your King!' (John 19:14)

Meditation

We do not need to be mystics to visualize the excruciating pain those long, razor-sharp thorns caused Our Lord. That this was one of the worst tortures in the unfolding of his Passion is easily understandable when we only have to remember our reactions when we suffer a mere pinprick on a finger. What could it have been like when three-inch thorns pierced his head? And this was just the physical agony: the mental anguish we can but guess at within the limits of our human imagination.

To complete Christ's humiliation, Pontius Pilate's soldiers took him into the Praetorium where the whole battalion stood waiting to insult and deride him. Imagine the scene in the large open square, hundreds of Roman soldiers ordered to witness and mock this blood-covered wreck of a man. They knelt before him, spat at him, and yelled out, 'Hail, king of the Jews' (Luke 19:3). Then they took the rod from his hand and beat him with it.

At last, even the soldiers had had enough, and removing his 'royal' cloak, they dressed him in his own clothes, and led him towards crucifixion. Yet among the Roman centurions, even during his lifetime, there had been glimpses of awe from a few of them, but most particularly the centurion who witnessed his crucifixion, and whom we know grace had touched, for at the very end he was heard to exclaim 'Truly this man was the Son of God!' And perhaps, this small incident was almost a prophetic, if not fully understood, realization that Christ was not just the Messiah of the Jews but the Saviour of all mankind.

Fourth Sorrowful Mystery

The Carrying of the Cross

So they took Jesus, and he went out, bearing his own cross, to the place called the place of a skull, which is called in Hebrew Golgotha.
John 19:17–18

While SS Matthew, Mark and John, relate something of Our Lord's torture before he was crucified, only St Luke describes these scenes of Jesus's sufferings in such detail, and traditionally it is believed that he obtained this information from Mary.

Some biblical experts and historians, experts on Roman customs, have said that so varied were methods of crucifixion that it is impossible to be certain whether Our Lord carried an entire cross, or parts of it. Other similar sources point out that two centuries before Jesus, it was Roman practice for the upright stake to be fixed in the ground and the prisoners left to carry the crossbeam which would then be attached to a vertical beam, a custom that indeed extended into Our Lord's time. From the point of view of the executioners in a region where crucifixion was the common method of death for criminals, it was obviously more hideously practical to have fixed vertical beams to which the crossbeam only needed to be attached.

This is confirmed by the eminent expert on the Shroud, Antonio Cassanelli, Secretary of the Giulio Ricci Diocesan Sindological Centre, who says that the crossbeam would have been attached across the shoulders, from right to left, by a rope, and that this procedure would have been carried out by an armed squad led by a centurion. The pain of this on a body already lacerated from the scourging would have been excruciating. Evidence on the Holy Shroud shows a large contusion, about 10cm by 9cm (4" × 3½") above the right shoulder-blade, made up of abrasions, one on top of another, and confirms that a heavy, rigid yet shifting object on the shoulder caused further injury which opened up the former abrasions. The wooden beam weighed about 40 kg.

This information about the form of the cross may be news to many people, but there is a fifteenth-century German painting at the Thyssen Boromisza Museum in Madrid which shows a busy, everyday scene in a market town, where in the foreground the local citizens go busily on their daily round, while in the far background a small figure – Our Lord – bearing a wooden crossbeam on his stooped shoulders, glances across at the people who are completely unaware of him as he staggers under the weight of his burden.

To add to their pain, prisoners on the way to crucifixion were whipped by soldiers or slaves. Maria d'Agreda, Anne Catherine Emmerich, and Teresa Neumann, in their private revelations, describe how ropes were attached to a belt around Jesus's body which were pulled by soldiers in front of him to hurry him along, and by others behind to pull him back, 'To vex and torment Him', this brutality making him fall not merely three, but several times. Evidence from the Shroud identifies micro-traces of earthly residues on the cloth, especially at the levels of the left knee, the foot, and the nose, which confirms that not only did the Man of the Shroud walk barefoot, but that he also fell down. This tallies with Teresa Neumann's account that new wounds were caused, especially to his knees, because the streets were paved with rough stones.

Anne Catherine Emmerich adds that the face of Jesus was swollen and wounded – which is borne out by the image on the Shroud which also shows that Jesus's nose had been broken.

Maria d'Agreda describes his body as looking like 'one continuous wound ... and in many parts of his shoulders the bones were laid bare and became plainly visible, all covered with blood.' Even the soldiers could see it was impossible for him to continue, so they called Simon of Cyrene to help carry the crossbeam.

When we read what St Luke tells us, that on the way to Golgotha 'there followed him a great multitude of the people, and of women who bewailed and lamented Him', we should remember that many of these were his fellow Jews, his supporters, who believed he was their Messiah; he was one of them. But those who cried 'Crucify him' were representative of the human race: the pagan population and those Jews influenced by the hostility and lethal jealousy of their all-powerful religious establishment, whose fear of unrest and consequent Roman retaliations induced them to curry favour with Pontius Pilate by declaiming that they wanted no other king but Caesar.

The mystics tell us about the sufferings of Jesus's mother, who followed her Son on his way to Calvary, accompanied by John and the holy women. Teresa Neumann described Mary as wearing a long bluish-grey cloak and a veil over her head, 'coarser material than our veils'. Teresa adds that when Our Lady was prevented from approaching him by the surging crowd, an angel guided the little group through a side-street, and mother and Son came face to face. Mary fell on her knees, but was brutally pushed aside by the executioners; looking into the eyes of her tortured son, did she recall how they used to gaze into each other's eyes – as mothers and babies do – when he was a tiny infant feeding at her breast? But the brief meeting is brought to an abrupt end as the crowd pushes forward, and in the crush, Our Lady sees Jesus fall.

Meditation

What must the condition of Jesus have been like when he started that walk to Golgotha – a walk that has been calculated as some 300 metres long? His entire body, from head to feet, was lacerated to such an extent that his bones were laid bare.

Tortured not just by physical pain but by interior anguish, and already aware of our apathy and ingratitude in the centuries of sin and misery yet to come, the Son of Man could have put an immediate end to his own sufferings had he so willed, yet instead chose to accept degradation for our sakes.

What must his mother have endured watching her Son's agony, understanding better than anyone else the extent of Christ's grief at man's wickedness? Witnessing the taunts and mockery, the violence and insults of the mob, as Jesus was dragged and pulled along the way to the cross, and she unable to help him, did Mary remember Simeon's prophecy all those years ago in the Temple?

'Behold this child is set for the fall and rising of many
　in Israel,
and for a sign that is spoken against
(and a sword will pierce through your own soul also)'
(Luke 2:34–5).

Christ did not have to go through this suffering; it was not for his sake but for ours that he did so. He did not die for the human species. He died for each individual, for you and me as unique souls.

Christ prayed, 'Father, if thou art willing, remove this cup from me; nevertheless not my will, but thine, be done' (Luke 22:42). We are not asked to seek pain, and all we can do when it comes is to throw ourselves on God's healing mercy and perhaps find the courage to offer up our sufferings for a special intention, or as penance for past sins, through once we have perfect contrition, have confessed them and received God's forgiveness, we should avoid dwelling on them. It is a temptation to think that God has not punished us as much as we deserve, and so we must punish ourselves in some way to make up for what he has left out; this, I understand, is a form of spiritual pride. Our Saviour is not a God of pain but a God of love.

As mentioned in an earlier chapter, when we place ourselves completely in the hands of God, it may be that the only way we can enter into a close relationship with him is for our cold, unfeeling hearts to be broken, in order that he can repair them and draw us closer to him. This may involve looking back at our past life and recognizing that many of the sorrows we have suffered – and perhaps inflicted – have sensitized our hearts and minds, so that we have reached a deeper understanding of the pain we may have caused to others, and are given the opportunity to pray for forgiveness retrospectively.

Fifth Sorrowful Mystery

The Crucifixion

And they brought him to the place called Golgotha (which means the place of the skull). And they offered him wine mingled with myrrh; but he did not take it. And they crucified him, and divided his garments among them, casting lots for them, to decide what each should take. And it was the third hour, when they crucified him. And the inscription of the charge against him read, 'The King of the Jews'.

Mark 15:22–5.

Cicero described crucifixion as the cruellest and most hideous of torments; no quick death here, but a long, lingering agony. This form of punishment had been imported from Phoenicia by the Greeks and Romans; it was not practised by the Jewish rulers who preferred their criminals to be stoned or hung from a gibbet, but those priests, scribes and elders who had called for Christ's crucifixion knew what it would entail.

According to various medical reports, although death was ultimately caused by suffocation because the posture of the body made it increasingly difficult to breathe, contributing causes may have been heart failure due to shock, exhaustion, thirst and loss of blood.

Jesus knew exactly what faced him as, in a state of collapse, he, Simon of Cyrene who was carrying the cross-beam, and the followers – executioners, wailing women, and the mob who came to mock – reached Golgotha on that first Good Friday.

Crucifixions were always held near busy highways, deliberately. The Roman authorities wanted the gruesome sight to be a lesson to criminals and troublemakers in general, and to the four soldiers who would carry out the execution.

Because of the finding from forensic tests on the Shroud, we may well have to revise our image of the cross. The eminent doctors and other scientific experts appointed to study it, in relation to what it reveals of the torture and crucifixion, have come to conclusions that have not yet reached the wider Christian community. The most startling of all is that the cross on which Our Lord was crucified could not have been the traditional Roman type – a horizontal beam fixed to a vertical one – because the bloody stains on that part of the Shroud where his arms had been attached to the wood prove that the damage done to them could only have been the result of their being brutally stretched up in a V-shape, forming the kind of cross seen on the back of Gothic chasubles.

Other significant evidence shows that in fixing his body to the cross, the executioners used three, not four, nails, one through each wrist (not the palms), and as the right foot was pressed against the vertical beam and the left foot placed over it, only one nail was driven through the two feet.

One expert has said there is also clear evidence that Christ's arms had been stretched so brutally that they were torn from their sockets. Furthermore, the angle of the way that the blood from his hands dripped on to his arms shows that the bloodstains on the Shroud could only have been made if the arms were fastened to a V-shaped cross.

This scientific evidence, which continues to be updated, corresponds yet again with the revelations from our four mystics, including the following examples:

- *St Bridget of Sweden*:

  'Then the cruel executioners seized Him and stretched Him on the cross. First they fixed his right hand to the beam which was pierced for the nails, and they transfixed His hand in the part which is firmest ... Now the cross was planted and its arms raised so that the junction of the Cross was between His shoulders, and the inscription board was fixed to the two arms rising above the head ...'

- *Catherine Emmerich*:

  'The whole Body of Our Lord had been dragged up and contracted by the violent manner in which the executioners had stretched out his arms ... Then they fastened his left foot to his right and having first bored a hole through them with a sort of piercer, they took a very long nail and drove it completely through both feet ...'

She goes on to say that when the left hand was pulled to the place prepared for it and nailed, the arms of Our Lord no longer fitted to the arms of the cross, which sloped upwards.

- *Teresa Neumann*:

  'When the executioners found it was impossible to drag the woollen garment which His Mother had woven for Him over His head, on account of the crown of thorns, they tore off this most painful crown, thus reopening every wound. He shook like the aspen as He stood before them ... when the executioners perceived that His left hand did not reach the hole they had bored for the nail, they tied ropes to his left arm and pulled the left hand violently until it reached the place prepared for it ... the whole body of Our Lord had been dragged up and contracted by the violent manner in which the executioners had stretched out His arms. The agony which Jesus suffered was indescribable ...'

- *Maria d'Agreda*:

'Then the executioners ordered the Saviour to stretch Himself on the Cross in order that they might mark the places where the holes were to be bored for the nails. The Saviour obeyed without a murmur, but the wicked men did not make the marks for the holes in the places corresponding with the dimensions of His Body but wider asunder in order to inflict upon Him a new and unheard-of martyrdom ...'

Coincidences across the centuries, long before the advent of forensic science?

Perhaps it was another coincidence that twelve years ago when I began research on the revelations of these mystics, across the world on another continent, Mel Gibson was doing the same thing. The results of his research were used in his magnificent film, *The Passion of the Christ;* I would urge all those who have not yet seen it to make every effort to do so.

Some Christians have said they couldn't possibly watch such a 'bloodthirsty' film; in short, they cannot bear the reality of what scourging and crucifixion entailed. Perhaps they would prefer a more sanitized presentation of the Passion, rather like the famous Velasquez painting of Christ on the Cross, which moving though it is, is a lie; no sign there of vicious scourging on that pale, pristine body with its neat spear-driven gash in the side of Jesus, and the tidy wounds on hands and feet, from which fall a few drops of blood. But far from exaggerating Christ's sufferings, in some scenes Mel Gibson underplayed them. For instance, he did not show Our Lord's skin being flayed to the bone during the scourging, nor his arms being wrenched out of their sockets to fit the cross. Both incidents mentioned not only by the mystics but in the evidence obtained from the Shroud. I *was* surprised that Jesus was depicted carrying a full cross rather than a cross beam, although Mel Gibson more accurately had the two criminals carrying a single beam apiece. And I imagine his reason for showing the crucifixions taking place high on a rocky hill, rather than close to a much-used busy road, as actually happened, had something to do with the former being more cinematically dramatic.

What is remarkable, is that over two thousand years after the event, the scourging and crucifixion of Jesus are stirring up the same anguish, fury and accusations as they did in AD 33, for Mel Gibson's film confronts the people of today with having to make up their mind between the three possibilities which faced the people of Christ's time: was he really the Jewish Messiah and Saviour of mankind, or was he a liar, or simply deluded? There was no alternative then, and there is no alternative now; only one of these possibilities is true.

During his physical torture on the cross, made worse by the cruel crown of thorns that dug into his head, Jesus was verbally attacked not just by the mindless mob but by the chief priests with the scribes and elders. 'He saved others; he cannot save himself. Let the Christ, the King of Israel, come down now from the cross, that we may see and believe.' (Mark 15:31–2)

And as his mother and his aunt, together with Mary Magdalene and John, stood by the cross, Jesus spoke those words that have echoed down the centuries: 'Woman, behold your son!' Then, to John: 'Behold, your mother!' (John 19:26–7)

In the final minutes before dying, Christ summoned up the last reserves of his strength, and first cried out with a loud voice in Aramaic: 'Eloi, Eloi, lama sabachthani?' 'My God, my God, why hast thou forsaken me?' (Mark 15:34) – the fulfilment of the prophecies contained in his ancestor David's heartrending Psalm 22. Then he gave another loud cry, and died. And at that moment the veil of the temple, a heavy curtain, was torn from top to bottom.

Meditation

By becoming man, Christ had made himself approachable to humanity at the deepest level of our needs, and as the ultimate proof of his love, he died for us. This new dimension of faith had been ratified at his final Passover when he said, 'This cup which is poured out for you is the new covenant in my blood' (Luke 22:20).

How many mothers throughout the history of the world who have watched their children in pain would gladly have borne the suffering themselves if it could be lifted from their loved ones? Most mothers. This, then, for Mary, was the sword Simeon had prophesied, being plunged to the hilt into her heart. Tradition has it that Our Lady suffered the agonies that Jesus experienced. One of the mystics, Catherine Emmerich, wrote that Mary suffered with inexpressible love and grief all the torments he was enduring.

Before his Passion had begun, had Jesus perhaps reassured his mother, that soon he would be back to console her? And she would, of course, believe him, because by then she understood fully who he was. But even so, living through the experience of his crucifixion was a reality, his suffering was a reality, and so was hers, recognized in the title given to her of Our Lady of Sorrows.

As for the high priests, scribes and elders, those who had come to jeer at his crucifixion, did any of them have moments of doubt? There had always been a lack of enthusiasm for the death penalty among the Jewish leaders; this is even mentioned in the Talmud, and when someone was sentenced to execution, four mounted guards always accompanied the condemned person to the place of execution, so that they could stop the proceedings if the judicial authorities gave a last-minute reprieve. So is it possible that, during Christ's crucifixion or afterwards, when they went away to their homes to prepare for the Paschal feast, some of them found it difficult to summon up the joy of Passover, and that the prayers of thanksgiving to God stuck in their throats, as the terrible question came into their minds: 'What if we were wrong?'

6

The Five Glorious Mysteries

First Glorious Mystery

The Resurrection

And when the sabbath was past, Mary Magdalene, and Mary the mother of James, and Salome, bought spices, so that they might go and anoint him. And very early on the first day of the week they went to the tomb when the sun had risen. And they were saying to one another, 'Who will roll away the stone for us from the door of the tomb?' And looking up, they saw that the stone was rolled back; for it was very large. And entering the tomb, they saw a young man sitting on the right side, dressed in a white robe; and they were amazed. And he said to them, 'Do not be amazed; you seek Jesus of Nazareth, who was crucified. He has risen, he is not here; see the place where they laid him. But go, tell his disciples and Peter that he is going before you into Galilee; there you will see him, as he told you.' And they went out and fled from the tomb; for trembling and astonishment had come upon them; and they said nothing to anyone, for they were afraid.

Mark 16:1–8

Although the Gospel accounts of the resurrection differ in details as would any event recounted by different people, some being more observant than others and all being of different temperaments, there is something particularly vivid about Mark's account. He makes it so easy for us to picture the very human reaction of the women on finding the empty tomb.

It may deepen our understanding of the atmosphere before the resurrection if we know something about Jewish mourning customs which date back to ancient times. When a Jewish person dies, their closest relatives – mother, father, sister or brother – sit shivah, a form of mourning which lasts seven days (that is what the Hebrew word 'shivah' means: seven). This practice even pre-dates the revelations on Mount Sinai, for Joseph mourned for seven days following the death of his father, the patriarch Jacob. But it was only after Moses had his momentous encounter with God on Mount Sinai that shivah was changed, by special decree, from being simply a general custom, to an obligation for all Jewish people, and this has continued into modern times.

An important purpose of the shivah is for family and friends to comfort the bereaved persons; not only by sharing their grief but also by helping to provide emotional healing. Each visitor approaches the mourners to offer condolences, and tears will inevitably be shed, but there will be comfort too in talking about the loved one who has died, and recalling happier times.

The shivah takes place at the home of the deceased or a close relative immediately after the interment. Food is prepared for the mourners by family or friends as the mourners themselves are not allowed to cook or carry out any household chores on the first day. The bereaved take their places on special mourning chairs, that is, chairs that have had their legs cut very short, giving them a curious stunted appearance. This is a modification of the original tradition when mourners would sit on the ground, perhaps on mats, pallets or even stools, and which may well have been the custom in the time of the Holy Family.

At sunset every day of the shivah, the practice is for a rabbi to come and lead the special mourning prayers, but first there must be a minyan, a gathering of at least ten men who must be present for the prayers. This is a Talmudic law which still prevails, and if there aren't enough men a swift call around is made to friends and neighbours to make up the numbers. But it is highly unlikely, though of course we cannot be sure about this, that there were any rabbis among the disciples, so one of the latter would have had to lead the prayers; their form depends on whether the deceased is a parent, child or sibling, but psalms are always included. Afterwards, refreshments are provided for the mourners and visitors. As noted in the Gospels, Jewish funerals are not allowed to take place on the sabbath, and this explains the haste with which Joseph of Arimathea, on the eve of the sabbath, asked Pilate to let him take away the body of Jesus. Then, together with Nicodemus, he prepared Christ's body with myrrh and aloes (about 100 lbs in weight) for burial on the Sunday.

As Mary and those who followed Jesus were devout Jews, swift arrangements would have been made so that after the religious entombment on the Sunday, a shivah would be held either at Mary's house or – seeing that Jesus had entrusted his mother to John – at the latter's home. In either case (and as Joseph, according to tradition, was not alive at the time, and Jesus was an only child) Our Lady would have sat alone in her bereavement.

However, as we know, it didn't quite turn out like that and any preparations for a shivah were overtaken by an unforeseen event: the resurrection.

As Mark tells us, very early that Sunday morning when it was still dark, Mary Magdalene, Salome and Mary the mother of James, went to visit the tomb, taking spices with them to anoint the body of Jesus.

When they arrived at the tomb the three women's relief, that somebody had already rolled away the huge stone closing off its entrance, quickly turned to alarm when they saw a white-robed stranger sitting there who told them not to be afraid. Easier said than done: the women were terrified. Matthew's account of this incident is more dramatic than Mark's: he tells us about 'a great earthquake; for an angel of the Lord descended from heaven and came and rolled back the stone, and sat upon it. His appearance was like lightning, and his raiment white as snow. And for fear of him the guards trembled and became like dead men' (Matt. 28:2–3). Those guards were the Roman soldiers placed outside the tomb to ensure that Christ's friends did not come and remove the body.

Can you imagine the scene when these women, scared out of their wits, rushed back to the grief-stricken apostles and disciples and told them what had happened? It is hardly surprising the women were not believed, and their story probably put down to hysteria or female emotionalism. But then Our Lord himself stepped in, appearing to two of the disciples when they were walking in the countryside.

It's rather satisfying to know that when these disciples returned to Jerusalem and told the apostles and their friends about their own incredible encounter with Jesus, they too were listened to with disbelief.

> So Jesus appeared to all eleven of the apostles as they sat at table, and reproached them for their obstinacy in not believing those who had seen him after his resurrection, saying, 'See my hands and my feet, that it is I myself; handle me, and see; for a spirit has not flesh and bones as you see that I have ...' And feeling normal human hunger, he said, 'Have you anything here to eat?' They gave him a piece of broiled fish, and he took it and ate it before them.
>
> (Luke 24:39, 41–43)

> Following this episode, Christ gave them his instructions which are as valid and urgent today as they were then: 'Go into the world and preach the gospel to the whole creation. He who believes and is baptised will be saved; but he who does not believe will be condemned.'
>
> (Mark 16:15–16)

Meditation

The enemies of God have always hated the truth, but perhaps never more so than in our own times where even some so-called Christians deny the reality of Christ's resurrection, and allege that this central event of Christianity should be taken not as fact but as symbolic of what we believe. This is absolute nonsense, as opposed to absolute truth. St Paul clarified the situation simply and for all time:

> Now if Christ is preached as raised from the dead, how can some of you say that there is no resurrection of the dead? But if there is no resurrection of the dead, then Christ has not been raised; if Christ has not been raised, then our preaching is in vain and your faith is in vain. We are even found to be misrepresenting God, because we testified of God that he raised Christ, whom he did not raise if it true that the dead are not raised. For if the dead are not raised, then Christ has not been raised. If Christ has not been raised, your faith is futile and you are still in your sins.
>
> (1 Cor. 15:12–17)

Belief in the bodily resurrection of Our Lord is binding on all Christians, and if anyone preaches otherwise, they preach falsehood.

The resurrection was not just a manifestation of God's omnipotent power; it was also a huge act of reassurance for us that should ease our natural fear of death. Above all, it should focus our minds on the state of our souls. This is a matter made all the more serious in our times by the assertions of some, who claim to believe in Christ, either that hell does not exist, or that it exists but nobody ever goes there.

Reflect then on Christ's own words:

> 'Enter by the narrow gate; for the gate is wide and the way is easy, that leads to destruction, and those who enter by it are many. For the gate is narrow and the way is hard, that leads to life, and those who find it are few.'
>
> (Matt. 7:13–14)

So we have it on the supreme authority that not only does hell exist, but, contrary to the declaration of those wishful thinkers who have only a passing acquaintance with the Scriptures, there *are*, tragically, 'many' condemned souls in that ghastly place. But we must recognize again that God does not condemn us; that is something we accomplish on our own by wilfully committing grave sin and then refusing to ask for his forgiveness which – together with his love – is always there for us, right to the very last seconds of our lives.

The marvellous prospects of heaven have never been better expressed than by St Paul:

> What no eye has seen, nor ear heard,
> nor the heart of man conceived,
> what God has prepared for those who love him.
> (1 Cor. 2:9).

Here again, is an example of how the Old Testament supplied the spiritual nourishment that fed the souls of the Jewish converts to Christ, for Paul's statement was a more eloquent paraphrase of Isaiah 64:4 –

> 'From of old no one has heard
> or perceived by the ear,
> no eye has seen a God besides thee,
> who works for those who wait for him.'

This promise implies a wonder-full heaven of endless fascination and enjoyment in the company of saints and in the presence of God; the exact opposite of dark hell's endless boredom, fury and chaos, in the loathed company of other damned souls, and the revolting (I use the word in both its meanings) presence of Lucifer. Who but a fool would choose the latter?

Yet in our politically-correct era of the third millennium, in the twenty-first century, Christ's message has been watered down. His instruction to the eleven disciples was unequivocal:

> And Jesus came and said to them, 'All authority in heaven and on earth has been given to me. Go therefore and make disciples of all nations, baptizing them in the name of the Father and of the Son and of the Holy Spirit, teaching them to observe all that I have commanded you; and lo, I am with you always, to the close of the age.' (Matt. 28:18–20)

Jesus did not tell his disciples that it would be prudent for them to leave out some nations because his teaching might upset them and be seen as an attack on their own forms of worship. *All* nations, was the divine command – command, not suggestion.

This is not to advocate the kind of fanatic and misplaced zeal of earlier centuries when people were persecuted and murdered because they refused to become Christian. Of course not. That violence to bodies and souls was the very antithesis of Christianity. Faith is a gift of the Holy Spirit, not to be forced upon anyone. The loving, merciful nature of Christianity and of Christians are what attract people to the truth and personal salvation.

Second Glorious Mystery

The Ascension

Then he led them out as far as Bethany, and lifting up his hands he blessed them. While he blessed them, he parted from them, and was carried up into heaven. And they worshipped him, and returned to Jerusalem with great joy, and were continually in the temple blessing God.

Luke 24:50–3

Following Christ's resurrection, his disciples would have been in a state of transcendent joy. Faith was no longer needed, for they had certainty. Their elation and excitement and the grace of the risen Lord's presence would have made them, in a sense, supernaturally receptive to all that he had to tell and teach during the forty days he would stay with them before his ascension; and while he was with them, he asked them to remain in Jerusalem to wait for the promise of the Father, which, he said, 'you heard from me, for John baptized you with water, but before many days you shall be baptized with the Holy Spirit'.

At this, they eagerly asked Jesus if this meant that he would restore the Kingdom to Israel. His reply must have puzzled them.

> 'It is not for you to know times or seasons which the Father has fixed by his own authority. But you shall receive power when the Holy Spirit has come upon you; and you shall be my witnesses in Jerusalem and in all Judea and Samaria and to the end of the earth.' And when he had said this, as they were looking on, he was lifted up, and a cloud took him out of their sight.
>
> (Acts 1:4–9).

As they stood gazing after him, two men in white robes stood next to them and asked why they were standing there looking into heaven.

> 'This Jesus, who was taken up from you into heaven, will come in the same way as you saw him go into heaven.' (Acts 1:11).

After this series of dramatic events which was transforming their lives and their destinies, they all returned to Jerusalem, as Jesus had told them to do, and they met together in an upper room where they were staying. They were all there (except the twelfth): 'Peter and John, James and Andrew, Philip and Thomas, Bartholomew and Matthew, James the son of Alphaeus, Simon the Zealot, and Judas the son of James, together with the women and Mary, the mother of Jesus, and with his brethren' (Acts 1:14), altogether about 120 people.

When they had settled down, Peter told them that the first thing they had to do was to choose another disciple who was a witness to Christ's resurrection and who would replace Judas, and they agreed that the choice should be decided by lot. One nomination was for a man called Joseph, who had been given the new name of Justus, and the other was for a man called Matthias. Then the gathering prayed, 'Lord, who knowest the hearts of all men, show which one of these two thou hast chosen to take the place in this ministry and apostleship from which Judas turned aside, to go to his own place' (Acts 1:24–5). The choice was for Matthias. So they were twelve again, the first bishops of the Church.

Meditation

What extremes of emotion the apostles had experienced since Good Friday to the Ascension: from deepest suffering to euphoria, and then, during the forty days before the Ascension, they had often been in the company of Christ who told them about the Kingdom of God, in preparation for (though they were still unaware of this) the spectacular events still to come.

They continued to hope that Israel's national splendour would be restored, though thinking about Christ's last words to them before his Ascension, they would have begun to realize that their mission to preach the Kingdom of God extended far beyond Jerusalem, Judea and Samaria: it was also to the ends of the earth and to all mankind; salvation was no longer restricted to the Jewish people, but was now accessible to everyone. But how could they possibly accomplish their mission when, apart from anything else, there was the basic practical problem of not being able to speak any foreign languages; so how could they go to the ends of the earth when the people they would meet had no knowledge of Aramaic or Hebrew?

It is no wonder that they all gathered in an upper room and 'With one accord devoted themselves to prayer' (Acts 1:14), for they had no idea at all of what lay in store for them; but in community they threw themselves on God's mercy and put themselves at his disposal. And here we come to a vital point: Mary was with them.

During those forty days on earth, Mary would have been the happiest of all the happy people with Jesus. Such love would have flowed between her and her Son; love that continues in heaven and hungers to embrace all mankind. What a blissful reunion they must have had, with all the grief of the Passion consoled. Perhaps it was during this period that Christ would have told Mary that, from the beginning of time, she had been chosen to be his mother, the Immaculate Conception. There was so much for them to talk about, many things that were still hidden from the Apostles, perhaps, and certainly still hidden from us. But at this stage Mary may still have been unaware of the role she was destined to play in the Kingdom of heaven, though Jesus must have been gently leading her to the realization that she was to be our spiritual mother and instrumental in our salvation.

The depths of her personal prayers following the Ascension would have been a natural combination of intense love and concentration on her beloved Son. What better model for our own contemplative meditation?

Third Glorious Mystery

The Descent of the Holy Spirit

When the day of Pentecost had come, they were all together in one place. And suddenly a sound came from heaven like the rush of a mighty wind, and it filled all the house where they were sitting. And there appeared to them tongues as of fire, distributed and resting on each one of them. And they were all filled with the Holy Spirit and began to speak in other tongues, as the Spirit gave them utterance.

Acts 1:2–4

This was the day when the Church was founded, and it began in that upper room, Peter and John, James and Andrew, Philip and Thomas, Bartholomew and Matthew, the other James and Simon, Judas, the son of James, and Matthias, the replacement for Judas Iscariot. So there they all were, the apostles – the first bishops; the evangelists, disciples, and Mary.

That evening, they sat waiting, and praying fervently, not knowing what to expect. But Mary, so close to her Son, may have had a good idea of what was about to happen, for the depths of Our Lady's prayers to Jesus, being both spiritual and maternal, were on a unique plane, and it is unlikely that the apostles had yet fully grasped that the very founding of the Church had depended on her co-operation.

Suddenly, they were galvanized at the sound of that mighty wind and the strange appearance of what seemed to be some form of fire above each of them. Christ's promise to them before his Ascension had been fulfilled in the most sensational and visible way, imbuing them with all that they would need to carry out his mission 'to the end of the earth' (Acts 1:8).

It must have been something of a relief to them that one of the first fruits of this miracle was that they had become instant expert linguists, and news of this obviously ran like wildfire among all the people who had come to Jerusalem, devout Jews from every country under heaven, who quickly went to see what all the fuss was about. So astonished were they to find the apostles speaking in their languages that some of them muttered to each other, 'Are not all these who are speaking Galileans? And how is it that we hear each of us in his own native language ... what does this mean?' When a few of those present accused the apostles of being drunk, Peter stood up and rebuked them; 'These men are not drunk, as you suppose, since it is only the third hour of the day' (Acts 1:15), and then he delivered his mighty speech to the assembled people, which still resonates with his impassioned fervour in proclaiming the ancient prophecy of Joel:

> 'And in the last days it shall be, God declares,
> that I will pour out my Spirit upon all flesh,
> and your sons and your daughters shall prophesy,
> and your young men shall see visions,
> and your old men shall dream dreams ...
> And I will show wonders in the heaven above
> and signs on the earth beneath,
> blood, and fire, and vapour of smoke;
> the sun shall be turned into darkness
> and the moon into blood,
> before the day of the Lord comes,

the great and manifest day.
And it shall be that whoever calls upon the name
   of the Lord shall be saved.'

                                        (Acts 2:17–21)

It was, in fact, the first papal pronouncement of the Church, and three thousand souls were baptized on that day alone.

Meditation

Most of those converts were Jewish, and once they had been baptized, they devoted themselves completely to spreading the teaching of the apostles, and the breaking of bread in each other's houses, in other words, the early form of Mass. Day by day there were more conversions and soon the apostles began to perform miracles.

What was so brave about the apostles is that they preached the Gospel in the temple, right in the very heart of Judaism. One can only imagine the shock felt by the priests, scribes and elders to observe the surge of conversions. Nothing had prepared them for the terrible possibility that once Christ had been crucified, it would not be a case of 'out of sight, out of mind'.

I wonder how many people, if asked, could immediately give the names of all twelve apostles? Shamefully, before writing this book, I certainly couldn't, nor had I ever fully appreciated the continual strains they would have suffered in the physically exhausting, and mentally demanding, lives they led spreading the Gospel in so many parts of the world. What hardships they suffered! Among the many countries where they preached the Kingdom of God, Thomas also went to India and Burma; Matthew to Ethiopia and Iran; Bartholomew to Armenia; Simon to Syria. James the Great went twice to Spain, where pilgrimage routes all lead to the great Cathedral of Santiago de Compostela in Galicia, which millions of pilgrims visit every year, and where the saint's bones are believed to be contained in a small ossuary behind the high altar.

The more one learns about these extraordinary men, the more love, respect and awe one feels at all they accomplished, and how impossible it would have been without the gifts of the Holy Spirit given to them at Pentecost. Of those twelve, only John and perhaps Matthew were to die a natural death. The rest were martyred by various hideous means: Peter, Andrew and Philip were crucified; Simon was mutilated; Jude was impaled; Matthias and James the Less were stoned; Thomas was stabbed; James the Great was decapitated, and Bartholomew was flayed and crucified. At the time of their martyrdom, Matthew and Philip were in their nineties.

There are still bishops in some countries in the world whose lives are in constant danger from the enemies of Christ; many potential martyrs spreading the Gospel, far away from the superficial 'civilization' of modern Western cities; thousands of missionary priests still labouring quietly and effectively in countries ruled by corrupt tyrants, where the poverty-stricken lives of the people have not improved over the centuries. These bishops and priests are the true heirs of the twelve apostles, and if the world is to be re-converted, please God, send us more of such men.

Mary's unique connection with the founding of the Church was to grow and continue in heaven, where at last the apostles would realize her key role in God's plan for our salvation. And so she continues, the mother of the Church and special protector of priests.

Fourth Glorious Mystery

The Assumption

'Who is this that looks forth like the dawn,
fair as the moon, bright as the sun,
terrible as an army with banners?'

Songs of Songs 6:10

There is a sense in which the Blessed Virgin Mary represents what humanity would have been like if it had not been distorted by original sin, and why she is often referred to as the second Eve, for Our Lady's assent to Gabriel at the Annunciation was the crucial first step towards the Incarnation. Not only do *we* have a debt of gratitude to her, but so does all of heaven, and Mary's glorious Assumption is an acknowledgement of this.

Critics point out that there is no mention of the Assumption in the Scriptures, though the above quotation from the Song of Songs could not be more prophetically apposite to Our Lady's role in heaven. The same critics also claim that the Assumption was added on to the deposit of faith in fairly modern times. In fact, it is thought to have been celebrated in the Western Church as early as the fifth century – possibly even earlier – but most certainly by AD 650. An English saint, Bishop Aldhelm of Sherborne referred to the Assumption as Our Lady's birthday in heaven, and it was during his lifetime that another saint, Pope Sergius, ordered its solemn observance and a procession in Rome. Later, in AD 847, a third saint, Pope Leo IV, added the vigil.

In the eighteenth century, Pope Benedict XIV declared that the denial of the Assumption would be 'impious and blasphemous', and over the following years there was an increasing number of petitions to the Holy See for a defining of the dogma. But it was not until 1946, after the Second World War, that Pius XII asked all the bishops of the Church for their opinion on the proposed dogma: the result was overwhelmingly in favour. In response, the

Pope said, 'This showed us what was the common faith of the Christian people, which faith the same authority upholds and directs. This common consent is of itself an absolute certain proof, which admits of no error, that the privilege is a question of truth revealed by God, and one contained in that divine deposit which Christ entrusted to His Bride to be faithfully guarded and infallibly proclaimed.' Rome had spoken, and after four more years of prayer, reflection and study, Pius XII solemnly defined the dogma of the Assumption of the Blessed Virgin Mary, on All Saints' Day, 1950.

The dogmatic definition states, 'The ever Virgin Mary, having completed the course of her earthly life, was assumed body and soul into heavenly glory.' What it does not state is whether Our Lady was assumed into heaven as a living person, or whether she first died and was then assumed body and soul into heaven.

There is no record of where she was living at the time of the Assumption. Some sources say it was in Ephesus where John had lived and died, but there is more support for the tradition that she had returned to Jerusalem. Both the Church of the Dormition on Mount Zion, and another church near Gethesemane, have been named as sites where she was buried, though no tomb has ever been found.

However, Pius XII made it clear that the question of whether she died before the Assumption or did not die, was *terra incognita*, and the faithful are not bound to either view. But that has not stopped speculation over the centuries, and while those who believe Mary first died and was entombed before her Assumption appear to be in the majority, many others believe that there was no death and that Our Lady was assumed directly into heaven at a moment chosen by Christ. And why not? Pope Alexander III said, 'Mary did not only give birth without pain, but also left the world without corruption, according to the angel's word, or rather of God through the angel, so that she could show herself full of grace and not partially full of grace.'

Surely, say those people who argue that as Jesus died before his resurrection, and Mary was not divine, she must have suffered bodily death before her Assumption. This ignores two important points: Our Lord did not die of sickness or old age; he died (or rather, was murdered) as an act of sacrifice for us; he allowed himself to be murdered, to take on our sins. Our Lady, however, was born Immaculate and therefore death had no dominion over her, so why is it not likely that her son had already told her of his plans for her Assumption before his own Ascension into heaven, and that when the time came, he sent angelic messengers, or even came himself for his beloved mother, and in the twinkling of an eye, faster than light, in her Son's embrace, she found herself in heaven?

Meditation

What joy and excitement there must have been in heaven at the Assumption, an event the angels, archangels, and the souls of the redeemed had been awaiting expectantly in that dimension of bliss which we can only glimpse through a glass darkly. And for Mary, what glorious surprises awaited her as Jesus revealed his continuing plan for mankind's salvation, the battles still to be fought against evil, and – most particularly – how crucial her participation would be as his mediatrix of all graces, the creature most feared and hated by Lucifer and his dark minions.

From the moment of the Annunciation, this unassuming young Jewess had posed a terrible threat to the powers of wickedness, and now with her Assumption, Mary had become their greatest enemy in the battle for souls, 'Terrible as an army with banners'. The words 'Bright as the sun' would also acquire special significance at Fatima in 1917, when the sun seemed to spin during the apparition of Mary as Our Lady of the Rosary. Her power lies in the devastating strength of her humility and trust in God. She is our shining example.

Fifth Glorious Mystery

The Coronation of Our Lady

And a great portent appeared in heaven, a woman clothed with the sun, with the moon under her feet, and on her head a crown of twelve stars.

Rev. 12:1

Although there is no scriptural basis or infallible doctrine regarding the Coronation of Our Lady, the title 'Queen of Heaven' is one of the oldest to be bestowed on Mary and confirms a tradition that goes back to the earliest centuries of the Church; it is also a logical sequel to the scope of Our Lady's power and influence in heaven given to her by God following the Assumption.

As Queen of Heaven (and given that Christ, as royal Messiah, was directly descended from King David, she is sometimes referred to as Queen Mother) Mary is our heavenly mother, whose role is based on merciful love.

In the document *Lumen Gentium*, issued by the Second Vatican Council, the chapter on Our Lady refers to her as the temple of the Holy Spirit, and continues: 'Because of this gift of sublime grace she far surpasses all creatures, both in heaven and on earth.' There is also a thought-provoking comment about the gradual unfolding of God's plan for our salvation:

> The books of the Old Testament describe the history of salvation, by which the coming of Christ into the world was slowly prepared. The earliest documents, as they are read in the Church and are understood in the light of a further and full revelation, bring the figure of a woman, Mother of the Redeemer, into a gradually clearer light. (*LG* 55).

This implies that over time we shall come to understand more fully the extent of God's continuing plan for Our Lady's part in our salvation.

Lumen Gentium emphasizes that the Blessed Virgin is

invoked in the Church under the titles of Advocate, Helper, Benefactress, and Mediatrix, and adds: 'This however, is so understood that it neither takes away anything from nor adds anything to the dignity and efficacy of Christ the one Mediator.'

Mary is our reason for being proud of our creaturehood because, herself a creature, she has been crowned in heaven above all the angels and saints. Unique on earth, she is also unique in heaven.

It was Pope Pius XII who instituted 31 May as the feast day of Mary, Queen of Heaven, and it took the place of what hitherto had been the feast known as Mary, Mediatrix of All Graces, though the new feast was designed to emphasize Mary as mediator. (Later, in 1969, with the reform of the liturgical calendar, the date was changed to 22 August.) Then, at the height of the Second World War, the Holy Father took a step which perhaps has not been sufficiently appreciated by the vast majority of Catholics: on 31 October 1942, he consecrated the world to the Immaculate Heart of Mary, Mother and Queen. The consecration formula drew attention to a significant parallel: 'As the Church and the entire human race were consecrated to the Sacred Heart ... so we in like manner consecrate ourselves forever also to you and your Immaculate Heart, our mother and queen of the world, that your love and patronage may hasten the triumph of the kingdom of God.'

There is much food for thought here because the Pope understood (perhaps better than anyone living at the time) that the war being fought was not just a physical one but a spiritual one too, with a raging battle between civilization and the principalities and powers involved in the Nazis' malevolent, anti-God reign of terror. And knowing Lucifer's hatred for Our Lady, it was a brilliant spiritual strategy on the part of Pius XII to name her not just as the Immaculate Heart but also Queen of the world, which magnified her power and influence as Queen of Heaven.

Earthly queens come and go, and always retain a certain distance from their subjects, whereas Mary, crowned by her Son, is always there for us, at a prayer's distance.

Lumen Gentium beautifully sums up the bond between the people of the Church and Christ's mother:

> The faithful still strive to conquer sin and increase in holiness. And so they turn their eyes to Mary who shines forth to the whole community of the elect as the model of virtues. Devoutly meditating on her and contemplating her in the light of the Word made man, the Church reverently penetrates more deeply into the great mystery of the Incarnation ... Having entered deeply into the history of salvation, Mary, in a way, unites in her person and re-echoes the most important doctrines of the faith. (*LG* 65).

Meditation

Here is an intriguing yet little-known fact that may surprise many readers. In 1950, the Council of Europe held a competition for the design of the European flag, and an artist from Strasbourg, Arsène Heitz, who had been reading a history of the apparitions of the Blessed Virgin in the Rue du Bac, Paris, which led to the Miraculous Medal, felt inspired to design a flag using the symbols of a crown with twelve stars as mentioned in the quotation heading this chapter. She designed it against a blue background representing the mystery of the Immaculate Conception which coincided that year with the date which brought the Marian Year to its close. This turned out to be the winning entry, and we are all now familiar with the European flag – a flag designed with Mary in mind. Yet even as I write this, in Europe, the continent founded on Christianity, the politicians refuse to include any mention of God in the proposed European Constitution. The Holy Father has publicly expressed his profound dismay at this. So in our meditation on this Mystery, we may wish to ask Our Lady, Queen of Heaven, for her powerful intercession that this godless decision may be overturned.

7

The Five Mysteries of Light

First Mystery of Light

Jesus is Baptized in the Jordan

Then Jesus came from Galilee to the Jordan to John to be baptized by him. John would have prevented him, saying, 'I need to be baptized by you, and do you come to me?' But Jesus answered him, 'Let it be so now; for thus it is fitting for us to fulfil all righteousness.' Then he consented. And when Jesus was baptized, he went up immediately from the water, and behold, the heavens were opened and he saw the Spirit of God descending like a dove, and alighting on him; and lo, a voice from heaven, saying, 'This is my beloved Son, with whom I am well pleased.'

Matt. 3:13–17

We do not know whether the two cousins, Jesus and John, met while they were growing up, Jesus in Nazareth, and John in Ein Karem: perhaps not often because of the long travelling distance between the two places. But it is reasonable to think that the families may have met at least during Passover, when everyone went up to Jerusalem for the temple celebrations, though they probably lost touch when the elderly Zechariah and Elizabeth died, and John embarked on his life, a life that had been prophesied by Isaiah: 'Prepare the way of the Lord, straighten out his paths ...'

The appearance of John the Baptist came at a time when there was growing expectation and impatience among the Jewish people for freedom from the yoke of Rome. Over the past few years false messiahs had arisen claiming they would accomplish this, but their grandiose plans were failures. Only a few people, close relatives of the Holy Family, might have remembered the miraculous events surrounding the birth of Jesus, and the Family's escape into Egypt to avoid Herod's murderous plan to kill their son, but generally it would have meant little to the current generation.

John's fervour and eloquence about the Kingdom of God, and about the need for penitence, had touched a deep chord in the hearts and minds of the people who came from all over Jerusalem and the Judean countryside to confess their sins and be baptized by him. But he had no time for hypocrites, and when many Pharisees and Sadducees turned up for baptism, he called them a brood of vipers. 'Who warned you to flee from the wrath to come? Bear fruit that befits repentance, and do not presume to say to yourselves, "We have Abraham as our father"; for I tell you, God is able from these stones to raise up children to Abraham' (Matt 3:9). Just being Jewish was no guarantee of salvation.

The Baptist is often pictured as an unkempt man, rather wild of eye and hair, and covered with animal skins, but this is something of a distortion of the reality. First, though he spent so much time in the wilderness, he would have kept himself clean for that was a strict requirement in the Jewish code of personal hygiene. Second, he was not covered in camel skins, but in a long garment made of woven camel hair and tied with a leather belt. True he ate wild locusts and honey, but at the time, locusts were considered something of a delicacy, and everyone loved honey; there would have been berries, too, in the countryside. In other words, he lived off the land.

His striking appearance and charisma must have enthralled his listeners; 'I baptize you with water for repentance; but he who is coming after me is mightier than I, whose sandals I am not worthy to carry; he will baptize you with the Holy Spirit and with fire' (Matt. 3:11).

John knew the Messiah was among them, but it appears he did not immediately recognize Jesus as his blood relative, for he told the priests who had been sent to interrogate him that before Jesus came to be baptized he did not know him. But Jesus of course knew about John, because their two destinies had been intertwined from the beginning, even before their birth; and now, by the banks of the tree-shaded River Jordan, the paths John had been straightening out were about to intersect with the paths taken by Jesus, when he came and asked John to baptize him. Initially John hesitated, as he felt himself unworthy, but then Jesus made a significant comment to reassure John that they were complying with the biblical prophecies of the advent of the Messiah: 'Let it be so now, for thus it is fitting for us to fulfil all righteousness' (Matt. 3:15). And, later, to John's own disciples, Jesus emphasized the significance of the Baptist's role, putting him on the same prophetic footing as the great Hebrew prophet who foretold the coming of the Messiah; 'For all the prophets and the law prophesied until John; and if you are willing to accept it, he is Elijah who is to come. He who has ears to hear, let him hear' (Matt. 11:13–15).

Meditation

We have a great deal to ponder about in all the Mysteries of Light, because they help to deepen our spiritual insight into Christ's life during the three years he lived openly among men and women as the Messiah, and it was the baptism of Jesus which signalled the beginning of his public ministry. From that moment on, he emerged from the silent, secret years in the bosom of his family to reveal, at last, who he was. Mary and Joseph knew already (though some sources say that Joseph died shortly before Jesus began his public ministry) and we can only imagine the powerful emotions they must have experienced – trepidation, perhaps, as well as expectancy – when they heard that John the Baptist had announced that the Kingdom of God was at hand.

Once John understood his part in the coming of the Messiah, and eventually realized it was his own cousin, the blood bond as well as the spiritual one must have been a cause for joy to him, to Jesus and to Mary, who would then have been in her late forties or early fifties. John was family, and it would have been the most natural thing in the world for the Baptist to talk about his late parents to Mary, the one woman who had known them so well.

John's understanding of the divinity of Christ is apparent from the profound comment he made to his followers, 'Behold, the Lamb of God, who takes away the sins of the world! This is he of whom I said, "After me comes a man who ranks before me, for he was before me"' (John 1:29–30) – outside space and time.

If there had been such a hunger for a political messiah who would re-establish the nation as a great force, why, it may be asked, were people flocking to see and listen to Jesus and John, when they knew that what they were preaching had nothing to do with materialistic aspirations? But this is to forget that from infancy to old age, every aspect of Jewish lives was governed by their strict adherence to the laws of God as embodied in the Commandments given to Moses. They were indeed, the People of the Book, for the Old Testament was both their history and their Bible. It was their fidelity to God's commandments that distanced them from the pagan world within which they were forced to live.

Once settled in Canaan, they underwent a slow but steady transformation from being a nomadic people to a stable one, with families living in villages, towns and eventually cities. Over the centuries, there were frequent fallings away from their fidelity to God, yet after periods of turmoil, wars and dallying with paganism, they always returned to him. It can be said that the relationship between the Jews and God has always been a passionate one. But the spiritual basis of the Commandments became overlaid with a mounting series of petty rules and regulations which

distorted the beautiful simplicity of the original Commandments. Thus, when Christ and John preached about the true
Kingdom of God, they were reaching out and touching the
deepest recesses of Jewish souls. Naturally the Sanhedrin,
Pharisees and Sadducees regarded opposition to what they
saw to be their right to add to God's laws as an attack on
traditionalism. But Jesus made it abundantly clear in the
most scathing terms that this was a man-made legalism
rather than an authentic interpretation of the law. 'The
scribes and Pharisees sit on Moses' seat; so practise and
observe whatever they tell you, but not what they do; for
they preach, but do not practise. They bind heavy burdens,
hard to bear, and lay them on men's shoulders' (Matt.
23:2–4).

The relevance of Moses to the teaching of Jesus was
brought up again when the disciple, Philip, with great
excitement, told his friend, Nathanael, 'We have found
him of whom Moses in the law and also the prophets
wrote, Jesus of Nazareth, the son of Joseph' (John 1:45).

Jesus and John would never meet again in this world.
But right to the end of his life, before his beheading by
Herod, John would have been told all about his cousin's
miracles and works by various disciples. And when Jesus
heard about John's decapitation he would have mourned
deeply for that wonderful man. After this, Matthew tells
us, Jesus withdrew into Galilee.

Second Mystery of Light

The Miracle at Cana

*On the third day there was a marriage at Cana in Galilee, and the
mother of Jesus was there; Jesus also was invited to the marriage,
with his disciples. When the wine failed, the mother of Jesus said to
him, 'They have no wine.' And Jesus said to her, 'O woman, what
have you to do with me? My hour has not yet come.' His mother
said to the servants, 'Do whatever he tells you.'*

John 2:1–5

Not long after the meeting between Jesus and John the Baptist, Jesus left for Galilee again, and accompanying him were Philip and Nathanael; the latter was his most recent disciple, the one who had initially been doubtful about following Jesus, saying laconically about a place which was generally regarded as being peopled by dim-witted, and not very religious, yokels, 'Can anything good come out of Nazareth?' Yet it was to the home in Cana of this new apostle that Jesus had been invited to a family wedding.

As mentioned in connection with the first Joyful Mystery, Jewish weddings were very lively affairs that often went on for days. And though the bridegroom and his family in Cana may have thought they had provided sufficient food and wine for their guests – and it was always red wine, as white wine was virtually unknown at the time – it seems they had either miscalculated the quantity that would be consumed or, more likely under the circumstances, perhaps they could not afford a larger amount. Either way, dire embarrassment faced everyone if the flagons ran dry.

John tells us that there were six stone jars standing there filled with water for the Jewish purification rites. Jesus told the servants to fill them up to the brim. When they had done this, he told them to draw some out and hand it to the steward of the feast. This unlikely sommelier having tasted it and having no idea where it came from, called over the bridegroom and said to him, 'Every man serves the good wine first; and when men have drunk freely, then the poor wine; but you have kept the good wine until now' (John 2:10). And what wine! The rarest vintage in the world, past, present and future.

Meditation

What induced Jesus to produce his first miracle, which, superficially, had nothing to do with spreading the Kingdom of God, and which was kept secret from the bemused host and delighted guests, at a private wedding party?

This miracle has layers of significance; first let us

consider the opening sentence with which St John begins this chapter of his Gospel: 'On the third day there was a marriage at Cana ...' Some commentators point out that the Apostle uses these words to indicate a joyful symmetry with another third day and another, greater, miracle that was to come: the resurrection.

Then there is the very presence of Jesus at a wedding, a presence that would have showered many blessings and special graces on the newly-married couple, as it does on all sacramental marriages. There was not only plenty of wine at the wedding in Cana: there would also have been many families, friends, music, dancing, delicious food, and much laughter. Christ came to bring joy into the world, not sour-souled negation of all that has been created for our enjoyment.

Above all, it is in the answer to the question, Why did Jesus choose to produce such a miracle on such an occasion? that we encounter the significance before which all other reasons pale. He did it because his mother asked him to. It was before he was ready to reveal himself publicly as the Messiah, but his Imma (for that is the familiar version of the Aramaic word for mother, as Abba is for father) had urged him to help, and he simply could not refuse her. And what is more, she knew he would not refuse her. 'O woman what have you to do with me?' is as easy for us to misunderstand as was his response on the earlier occasion when as a boy he was found at the temple. Everything depends on language and expression, and we can be sure that Jesus's tone of voice was one of affectionate, if slightly exasperated, bantering, common among loving families. But Mary knew her Son, so she simply instructed the servants to do whatever he told them to do.

In this little episode, Christ demonstrates the power of his mother's influence over him, and that it is enough for him that she asks for a favour for it to be granted. The incredulous will ask, 'How can a mere creature have influence over God?' But Mary is not a mere creature: she is God's greatest created being, and even if this has been said before, it can never be repeated too many times, because with that power of hers she can help us in working towards our salvation.

There is also a biblical significance in Christ's use of the word 'Woman'. In St John's Revelation, when the apostle describes the battle between good and evil, he says: 'Then the dragon was angry with the woman, and went off to make war on the rest of her offspring, on those who keep the commandments of God and bear testimony to Jesus.' This is the woman to whom God has given such great influence in heaven and on earth.

Today, young Christian couples often choose the Church of the Miracle at Cana to celebrate their own weddings. This historic church is built on the remains of a sixth-century one and has a mosaic floor dating back to the fourth century.

Third Mystery of Light

Jesus proclaims the Kingdom of God

Now after John was arrested, Jesus came into Galilee, preaching the gospel of God, and saying, 'The time is fulfilled, and the kingdom of God is at hand; repent, and believe in the gospel.'

Mark 1:14–15

The moment had come. After his forty gruelling days and nights in the wilderness, tempted by the devil, lodging with wild beasts, but ministered to by angels, Christ was ready to reveal himself to the Jews as their Messiah and the Saviour of the world. And he went into Galilee to announce the Kingdom of God.

It started in an almost casual manner; walking along the shore of Galilee's beautiful lake (though it is often referred to as a sea), Jesus came across the two fishermen, Simon and Andrew, casting their net into the waters. 'Follow me,' he said to them, 'and I will make you become fishers of men' (Mark 1:17). Then going on a little further he approached two brothers, James and John, who were busy mending their nets; he called them too, and they left their father, Zebedee, in the boat with their hired servants.

Jesus attended the synagogue every sabbath day, so there would have been no surprise among the congregation at the Capernaum synagogue on that particular Saturday when he came in with a small group of fishermen. But there was astonishment when he stood up and began teaching them with an authority far superior to what they were used to from the scribes, rather as he had done as a young boy in the temple. And to add to the drama of the moment, there was sensational proof of who stood among them, for among the congregation there was a man possessed by an unclean spirit, who suddenly cried out, 'What have you to do with us, Jesus of Nazareth? Have you come to destroy us? I know who you are, the Holy One of God' (Mark 1:24). The worshippers in the packed synagogue must have been stunned at the turn of events during what would normally have been a routine sabbath religious service, and even more so when Jesus rebuked the unclean spirit possessing the man, and said, '"Be silent, and come out of him!" And the unclean spirit, convulsing him and crying with a loud voice, came out of him. And they were all amazed, so that they questioned among themselves, saying "What is this? A new teaching!"' (Mark 1:25–7).

From that day on, Jesus was in continual demand, healing minds, bodies and souls, teaching everyone he met the reality of God's kingdom, based on the interior life of the spirit and the personal relationship with God which this brings. But first, repentance of sins and a firm purpose of amendment to live in obedience to God's commandments according to the Law of Moses. For as he said, 'Think not that I have come to abolish the law and the prophets; I have come not to abolish them but to fulfil them. For truly, I say to you, till heaven and earth pass away, not an iota, not a dot, will pass from the law until all is accomplished.' (Matt. 5:17–18).

Meditation

The Kingdom of God was not a new religious concept introduced by Jesus: it was an eternal spiritual truth outside space and time. But for the purpose of our salvation, it had to be revealed by Jesus, as a man, in our world, at a precise point in history. And, at the same time, he had to gather together those people already known to God who would form the basis for the foundation and continuance of his Church. There could be no mistaking about the scope of the evangelization, for Jesus made it abundantly clear that there were to be no exceptions whatsoever of nations or races.

> 'All authority in heaven and earth has been given to me. Go therefore and make disciples of all nations, baptizing them in the name of the Father and of the Son and of the Holy Spirit, teaching them to observe all that I have commanded you; and lo, I am with you always to the close of the age.'
>
> (Matt. 28:18–20)

Christ made it clear, too, that faith is the gift of the Holy Spirit. Those first apostles were so successful because they embodied the humility, virtues and faith which rule out the kind of coercion and violence of later centuries when forced conversions caused so much damage to the reputation of the Church.

Over the centuries of wars, of exile, of foreign occupation of their land and of being surrounded by pagans, a spiritual tiredness had set in among the Jewish people which could only be bolstered up by fulfilment of the biblical prophecy of a Messiah; but what their priests and scribes failed to detect was a deep hunger for that special closeness to God which had been enjoyed by their patriarchs. The constant accretion of petty precepts imposed upon them, which led to hypocrisy and self-righteousness amongst those who made a public show of their prayers and giving of alms, was not conducive to a deep, meditative, interior faith. Indeed, an ancient saying expressed disdain for those 'who made for themselves the yoke of the Law easy and light', for unfortunately the aim of the rabbinic hierarchy was to make the yoke 'as heavy as possible', equating this with piety.

Imagine then the relief and joy of the people when they learnt from Jesus that his yoke was light, and the Kingdom of God was not a matter of applying to themselves a rigid set of pointless rules which had nothing to do with goodness, but rather of turning to God as children to their father, simply and humbly, asking for their needs, and keeping his commandments, because the Kingdom of God was within their own souls.

To re-read the teaching of Our Lord on the Kingdom of God in the Gospels is to experience the same sense of relief and gratitude that those first Christians would have experienced. It should also help us to a fuller understanding of the importance that no 'dot' or 'iota' be added to Christ's two straightforward and beautiful commandments, which encapsulate all the other commandments. 'You shall love the Lord your God with all your heart, and with all your soul, and with all your mind. This is the great and first commandment. And a second is like it, You shall love your neighbour as yourself. On these two commandments depend all the law and the prophets' (Matt. 22:37–40).

Fourth Mystery of Light

The Transfiguration

And after six days Jesus took with him Peter and James and John his brother, and led them up a high mountain apart. And he was transfigured before them, and his face shone like the sun, and his garments became white as light. And behold there appeared to them Moses and Elijah, talking with him. And Peter said to Jesus, 'Lord, it is well that we are here; if you wish, I will make three booths here, one for you and one for Moses and one for Elijah.' He was still speaking, when lo, a bright cloud overshadowed them and a voice from the cloud said, 'This is my beloved Son, with whom I am well pleased; listen to him.' When the disciples heard this, they fell on their faces, and were filled with awe. But Jesus came and touched

them, saying, 'Rise, and have no fear.' And when they lifted up their
eyes, they saw no one but Jesus only.

Matt. 17:1–5

That the Transfiguration took place on a high mountain, we know, but there is still uncertainty as to whether it happened on Mount Hermon, to the north of Caesarea Phillipi with breathtaking views across to Lebanon, the Jordan Valley, the Dead Sea and even as far as Jerusalem; or on Mount Tabor in southern Galilee on the Plain of Esdraelon, just over five miles from Nazareth. But as even the lowest peaks of the former are some 9,000 ft high, and the latter under 2,000 ft, tradition favours Tabor. This makes more sense than the theory that Jesus led his closest disciples, Peter, John and James, on an expedition up a mountain with rocky ravines and other dangerous features that would have involved many hours of climbing up and coming down.

There is another reason why Tabor seems the better candidate: it has a huge plateau on the top measuring 1,239 yards long and 411 yards wide which has been described as looking like an altar inviting worship. Both mountains are mentioned in Psalm 89, written about 1,000 years before the Transfiguration:

The heavens are thine, the earth also is thine;
the world and all that is in it, thou hast founded them.
The north and the south, thou hast created them;
Tabor and Hermon joyously proclaim thy name.

Initially, Peter, John and James appeared to have no idea why the Master was taking them up the mountain, and when they reached the top, they were so exhausted that they fell asleep. But when Jesus began to pray, they apparently woke up and saw Jesus in all the glory of his Transfiguration: his whole appearance had undergone a complete change, as though he were illuminated from within; 'dazzling white', according to Luke (9:29) 'intensely white' according to Mark (9:3). As the apostles watched all this in fear and trembling, two men appeared and talked to Jesus about his death that was to take place in Jerusalem, and from their conversation and appearance, Peter realized who they were. His state of extreme nervous tension is clearly conveyed in Matthew's account; he tells us that Peter suddenly burst out, 'It is well that we are here; if you wish, I will make three booths here, one for you and one for Moses and one for Elijah' (Matt. 17:4).

The relevance of Peter's offer needs to be seen against the likelihood that the Transfiguration took place in early autumn during the festival of Sukkah, one of the holiest in the Jewish liturgical year, and attended by Jewish pilgrims from all over the known world. It was (and still is) a week-long festival that commemorates the exodus from Egypt when, during their forty years of wandering through the wilderness, families would build booths for themselves to shield them from the hot desert sun. In the time of the Holy Family, every family would erect an open leafy 'booth' which had to be made from tree boughs, where they would eat, sleep, study and pray, and on the night before the end of the festival, there would be a solemn dedication before God against heathenism.

Thus, Peter's spontaneous offer to build booths for Jesus and his two heavenly visitors was a natural gesture of courtesy to the honoured guests from another dimension. But hardly were the words out of his mouth, when a bright cloud suddenly overshadowed them from which a voice was heard: 'This is my beloved Son, with whom I am well pleased. Listen to him' (Matt. 17:5). At which, the disciples fell on their faces in worship, until Jesus came over and gently touching them, said 'Rise, and have no fear.' And when they looked up, they saw he was by himself.

As the little group made their way down the mountain, Jesus commanded them, 'Tell no man the vision, until the Son of man is raised from the dead.' And the curious disciples asked him, 'Then why do the scribes say that first Elijah must come?' to which Jesus replied, 'Elijah does come, and he is to restore all things; but I tell you that Elijah has already come, and they did not know him, but did to him whatever they pleased. So also the Son of man will suffer at their hands' (Matt. 17:9–12). It was then that Peter, James and John understood that Jesus was referring to John the Baptist.

Meditation

The Transfiguration of Jesus is unlike any other part of the Gospels; it seems to stand alone, an episode almost outside the main narrative of the Apostles' account of Christ's time among them. He did not preach the Kingdom of Heaven on Mount Hermon, nor did he perform any miracles. But on that mountain, earthly limitations of space and time had been overcome for the participants and spectators at that meeting; it was a theophany, a manifestation of Christ's divinity.

What is of overwhelming significance about the event is that it was the only time during his earthly life that Jesus was seen in his glorified state, his divinity. And he was seen as the unifying Christ between Elijah, symbolizing the prophets, and Moses symbolizing the Law. It was a restatement of God's will for human salvation and for the eventual role in it of the Jewish people. The tragedy of their leaders refusing to acknowledge this did not cancel God's will for Israel to accept its Messiah, it only postponed it, for as prophesied by St Paul in Romans: 'I ask then, has God rejected his people? By no means! I myself am an Israelite, a descendant of Abraham, a member of the tribe of Benjamin' (11:1). And later in Romans, 'For if their rejection means the reconciliation of the world, what will their acceptance mean but life from the dead?' (11:15) ... 'But as regards election they are beloved for the sake of their forefathers. For the gifts and the call of God are irrevocable' (11:28–29).

The tone of Romans 11 is something of a rebuke by St Paul to those gentile converts who, having received the gift of faith, think this gives them the right to look down on the Jews. He emphasizes that the lack of belief among the Jewish communities at large is only temporary, and in due course, they will all recognize Christ as their Messiah which will bring great blessings to the world. 'For if you have been cut from what is by nature a wild olive tree, and grafted, contrary to nature, into a cultivated olive tree, how much more will these natural branches be grafted back into their own olive tree .... and so all Israel will be saved' (Romans 11:24,26).

This prophesied destiny of the Jewish people continues to develop, gathering momentum in an era when Jewish conversions to the Faith are growing slowly but steadily, while apostasy increases among the gentiles. As early as the fourth century, this was foreseen by St John Chrysostum who said, 'Seeing the gentiles abusing little by little their grace, God will recall the Jews a second time.' And later in the seventh century, St Jerome said, 'Their sins occasioned the salvation of the gentiles and again the incredulity of the gentiles will occasion the salvation of Israel.'

But from the beginning there have always been malevolent forces, both spiritual and temporal, that arise in every generation to oppose God's plan for the final reconciliation of the Jews to Christ, which is closely identified with the salvation of all mankind. And it is from this spiritual perspective that we should be aware of Lucifer's most successful ploy against this: anti-Semitism. As we know, he hates all human beings, but he has a raging and personal hatred for the Jewish people, precisely because the Son of God chose to be born as a Jew, of a Jewish mother, and – the most wounding insult of all – God made the Jewess Mary the most powerful created being in heaven.

Those who fall into the poisonous trap of anti-Semitism, whether entire communities or individual people, place their own souls in peril, for they delay the Divine plan – a particularly foolhardy policy for those anti-Semites who mistakenly regard themselves as Christians and must bear the blame for the reluctance of Jewish people to recognize Christ: a grave responsibility which they will eventually have to justify personally to Our Lord. In this context, we should remember Pope John XXIII's moving prayer shortly before he died, 'Forgive us the curse we unjustly laid on the Jews. Forgive us that with our curse we crucified thee a second time.'

Meanwhile, in our Rosary prayers and meditation, we have the perfect opportunity to further God's plan for the conversion of the Jews and the consequent spiritual transfiguration of the world.

Above all, the Transfiguration calls our attention to the shining splendour of Christ's divinity, witnessed by those three fortunate disciples, who may have found strength in the memory of this miracle when his Passion began at Gethsemane. And in times when it often seems that the wicked are inheriting the earth, the significance of the Transfiguration provides us with a great spiritual tonic.

Fifth Mystery of Light

The Institution of the Eucharist

You shall observe this rite as an ordinance for you and for your sons for ever. And when you come to the land which the Lord will give you, as he has promised, you shall keep this service. And when your children say to you, 'What do you mean by this service?' you shall say, 'It is the sacrifice of the Lord's passover, for he passed over the houses of the people of Israel in Egypt, when he slew the Egyptians but spared our houses.' And the people bowed their heads and worshipped.

Exodus 12:24–7

And as they were eating, he took bread, and blessed, and broke it, and gave it to them, and said, 'Take; this is my body.'

Mark 14:22

Passover soars over all the other Jewish festivals, being as it is at the very heart of the people's nationhood and its identity with God's promise to them. In Israel, throughout its history, *Pesach* (to use its Hebrew name) has always been celebrated on one night only. In the diaspora, and among the ultra-Orthodox community, however, it is celebrated over two nights, though it never falls on a Saturday, as this would infringe the law against any work on the sabbath day, and there is great deal of work in the preparation of the Paschal feast.

There is an ancient tradition that men at the Passover table should lean to their left – not too onerous a rule in modern times, when the men sit on chairs at a table, where they can prop up their left elbow and lean on that hand. But in the time of Christ, each man was provided with a low divan and substantial cushions for support, so that he could recline easily on his left side around a low, long table (U-shaped to allow the guests to sit opposite each other) with his legs stretched out on the floor.

It was the custom for the host or head of the household, to have the chief guest not on his right, but on his left, probably because that would be the way the host would naturally be facing; at the Last Supper, everything indicates that it was Judas who was given (or perhaps claimed) this place of honour, while John sat to the right of Jesus. Biblical experts point out that when Jesus told the disciples that one of them was to betray him, and Judas asked 'Is it I, Master?' and Our Lord replied 'You have said so' (Matt. 26:25), the only way this exchange could have taken place without any one else knowing was if Jesus and Judas were in the closest proximity. Peter, sitting across the table from John, made some sort of gesture to him indicating he should ask Jesus who the traitor was, which he did. And Jesus replied, 'He who who has dipped his hand in the dish with me, will betray me' (Matt. 26:23).

This entire little episode passed unnoticed by the other disciples, and even when Jesus said to Judas, 'What you are going to do, do quickly' (John 13:27), and Judas left the room, they still had no idea about the sinister turn of events, and merely thought that as Judas was in charge of the money box, he had probably gone out to buy more provisions for the feast or to give alms to the poor.

Earlier, when Christ had gone down on his knees to wash the feet of his disciples in an act of supreme humility and love, Judas was included. What could he have been thinking, feeling, when he watched Our Lord going from disciple to disciple until he reached the place where he, the betrayer, sat, and looked down at the head of Christ bent over his feet to perform the cleansing rite? There was still time to change his treacherous decision, but he let the moment pass.

There was a terrible innocence about the apostles that night, for they still had not understood Christ's many hints of what he was about to undergo; but gently, step by step he led them deeper into the understanding of his – and their – destiny, beginning with his first touching words to them: 'I have earnestly desired to eat this Passover with you before I suffer; for I tell you I shall not eat it until it is fulfilled in the Kingdom of God' (Luke 22:15–16).

As the prayers and rituals of the evening ran their course, and Christ talked to them, the general trend of what he was saying began to disturb the Apostles, especially when he said, 'Where I am going you cannot come' (John 13:33), which elicited a puzzled response from Peter: 'Lord, where are you going?' (John 13:36), while Thomas backed this up, 'Lord, we do not know where you are going; how can we know the way?' (John 14:5). To which question, Jesus gave them – and all humanity – the answer:

> 'I am the way, and the truth, and the life; no one comes to the Father, but by me. If you had known me, you would have known my Father also: henceforth you know him and have seen him.'

But Philip wanted further clarification: 'Lord, show us the Father, and we shall be satisfied.' Jesus replied:

> 'Have I been with you so long, and yet you do not know me, Philip? He who has seen me has seen the Father; how can you say, "Show us the Father"? Do you not believe that I am in the Father and the Father in me? The words that I say to you I do not speak on my own authority; but the Father who dwells in

me does his works. Believe me that I am in the Father and the Father in me; or else believe me for the sake of the works themselves.'

(John 14:9–11)

What response could be more concise?

After the first part of the religious rite, the Passover meal is taken which celebrates the liberation from Egyptian slavery and the subsequent holy Covenant with God on Mount Sinai. But on this night, the Passover was to be like no other for it would establish a new covenant with God; no slaughtered lamb, but the Lamb of God to be led to the slaughter. And blood would be shed: his, for our salvation.

So Jesus took up a piece of the unleavened bread, blessed it, and broke it into pieces which would be handed to the disciples as part of the Passover rite, but then he added something different, something new, into the Hebrew liturgy, for he took a piece in his hands and said, 'This is my body which is given for you. Do this in remembrance of me' (Luke 22:19). After the meal, when the wine again had to be drunk from one cup, in accordance with the ritual, and which Jesus himself would have poured out and drunk before handing it round to them, he said, 'This cup which is poured out for you is the new covenant of my blood' (Luke 22:20). And with those words, the Last Supper became the first Mass.

Meditation

When Christ, breaking the unleavened bread at the Last Supper, said, 'Do this in remembrance of me', he did not mean that every time we eat an ordinary bit of bread it should be in remembrance of him. When the holy sacrifice of the Mass is celebrated in remembrance of Christ, it can only be called a sacrifice if the Eucharist is truly the Body of Christ, for without the Real Presence there can be no sacrifice. Although Christian denominations have various forms of Eucharistic services in remembrance of Our Lord's sacrifice, for a valid celebration of the Mass, remembrance in itself is not sufficient; the Host must be consecrated by a priest who has been ordained by a bishop in the direct line of the Apostles, and Communion taken only by those who believe in the Real Presence. Although this is taken for granted by Catholics, there is still confusion among many Christians about this, leading to a misunderstanding of what the Catholic Church means by the term 'unity'. Simply, the unity of the Church is the Real Presence in the Eucharist.

There are Christians who find belief in the Real Presence incomprehensible. How can a mere wafer become God's body? Yet they find no difficulty with the miracle that God became man and lived among us. Christ so loved and loves the world that, before his death on the cross, he made it possible for us to establish and continue in perpetuity a close relationship with him through his Presence in the Blessed Sacrament. It is also unique in that the Giver is himself the gift to us.

Christ humbled himself twice for our salvation: first by dying for us, and then by allowing himself to be contained within the apparent confines of what begins as a wafer until it is consecrated, and as a consequence he made himself vulnerable to the various attitudes, some more reverent than others, of those who administer and receive Communion.

Years ago, some time after I had become a Catholic, I dreamt that Jesus explained to me the significance of the Blessed Eucharist. Holding up the consecrated wafer, and looking gravely at me, he said, 'Do you know what this is? It is humility.' By this, I understood that this was the most humble thing he could do – to make himself available to us in the Blessed Sacrament. Since then, especially at Mass, I have been thinking about it a great deal – in other words, meditating on this priceless gift to us.

8

The (Possible) Future of the Rosary

'In my Father's house are many rooms.'
John 14:2

Recently there has been immense excitement about the landing on Mars of robotic probes, sent up by various space agencies; one of these probes is capable of lurching about the planet to collect rock and earth samples and of sending the information back to us. The main purpose of such experiments is to discover if there is, or ever was, some form of life on Mars. This search gained impetus a few years ago when a Martian meteorite found in the Antarctic, showed what could be fossils of tiny organisms. Now it is hoped that further exploration on Mars will be able to shed more light on this matter.

Another recent, and perhaps even more important discovery, is that there are other solar systems, many millions of light years away. 'Where does that leave your Christianity now?' non-believers ask delightedly. And even some Christians appear to be alarmed by the thought of life elsewhere. Yet, far from being worried, they should be overjoyed at proof of God's glory in the immensity of his creation.

'All well and fine,' the non-believers say. 'But you claim that Christ was crucified and resurrected on earth; what about other planets which might have human populations, perhaps even more developed than us, who have never heard of Christ?'

It was from an obscure region of a relatively unimportant part of the Middle East that Our Lord sent his disciples to preach his Gospel throughout the world. Is it not possible that God may have chosen our insignificant little planet, located on the outer rim of a huge galaxy, to be the Galilee of the cosmos? And that the time will come when a new generation of missionaries will spread the Gospel throughout the universe, and take their Rosaries along with them?

Bibliography

Bouquet, A.C. *Everyday Life in New Testament Times*, B. T. Batsford Ltd.

Bollone, Pierluigi Baima and Zacá, Stefano. *The Shroud Under the Microscope – Forensic Examination*, St Pauls (UK), 1998.

Caird, G.B. *The Apostolic Age*, Gerald Duckworth & Co. Ltd., 1955.

Cassanelli, Antonio. *The Holy Shroud*, Gracewing, Leominster and Nova Millennium Romae, Rome, 2002.

Connolly, Peter. *The Jews in the Time of Jesus*, Oxford University Press, 1994.

Consolmagno, Bro. Guy, SJ. *The Way to the Dwelling of Light – How Physics Illuminates Creation*, Vatican Observatory Foundation, 1998.

Corswant, W. *A Dictionary of Life in Bible Times*, Hodder & Stoughton Ltd., 1960.

Daniel-Rops, *Daily Life in Palestine at the Time of Christ*, Weidenfeld & Nicolson, 1962.

De Montfort, St Louis. *The Secret of the Rosary*, Montfort Publications, New York.

Deen, Edith. *Family Living in the Bible*, Spire Books, 1969.

Edersheim, Revd Dr. *Jewish Social Life*, The Religious Tract Society, London, c.1876.

— *The Life and Times of Jesus the Messiah*, vol.2, Longmans Green & Co., 1900.

Fitzmyer, Fr. Joseph A. SJ. *The Letter to the Romans*, Jerome Biblical Commentary, vol. 2. Prentice Hall, Inc., New Jersey, USA, 1968.

Ganzfried, Rabbi Solomon. *Code of Jewish Law* (tr. Hyman E. Goldin, LLB), Hebrew Publishing Co., Brooklyn, NY, 1961, 1963.

Everyday Life in Bible Times, National Geographic Society, 1967.

Ghiberti, Giuseppe. *Shroud, Gospels and Christian Life*, St Pauls (UK), 1998.

Godfrey, Fr, OFM. *The Holy Land*, Palphot Ltd., Herzlia, Israel.

Gollmick, I. E. D. *Customs and Costumes in Bible Days*, Bible Days and Bible Ways, Bedfordshire, 1975.

Holy Family in Egypt, The, Egyptian Ministry of Tourism, 1999.

Manelli, Stefano, FFI. *All Generations Shall Call Me Blessed*, Academy of the Immaculate, New Bedford, Mass.

Miller, Madeline S. and J. Lane Miller. *Encyclopedia of Bible Life*, Harper & Brothers, 1944.

O'Connell, Revd Patrick, BD (Columban Fathers, Ireland) and Carty, Revd Charles (Radio Replies Press Society, St Pauls, Minn.). *The Holy Shroud and Four Visions*, Tan Books and Publishers Inc., Rockford, Ill, 1974.

Orchard, Dom Bernard, OSB. *Born To Be King*, Ealing Abbey Scriptorium.

Payesko, Robert. *The Truth about Mary*, 3 vols., Queenship Publishing, Santa Barbara, Cal.

Polkinghorne, John. *The Way the World Is – The Christian Perspective of a Scientist*, Triangle, SPCK, 1983, 1992.

Ruffin, Bernard. *The Twelve – The Lives of the Apostles after Calvary*, Our Sunday Visitor Publishing Division, USA, 1984, 1997.

Scannerini, Sylvano. *Myrrh, Aloes, Pollen and Other Traces – Botanical Research on the Shroud*, St Pauls (UK), 1998.

Stannard, Russell. *The God Experiment*, Faber & Faber, 1999.

Tresmontant, Claude. *The Hebrew Christ – Language in the Age of the Gospels*, Franciscan Herald Press, Chicago, IU.

Vail, Anne. *The Story of the Rosary*, Fount, 1995.

Van Deursen, Dr A. *Illustrated Dictionary of Bible Manners and Customs*, Marshall, Morgan & Scott, 1958.

Wilkins, Eithne. *The Rose Garden*, Gollancz, 1969.

Wilkinson, John. *Jerusalem as Jesus Knew It*, Thames & Hudson Ltd., 1978.

Biblical texts are from the Catholic Edition of the Ignatius Revised Standard Version of the Holy Bible.